First published in 2015 by
Clarity Media Ltd
www.clarity-media.co.uk

Puzzles created by Dan Moore & Amy Smith
Design and layout by Amy Smith

About Clarity Media

Clarity Media are a leading provider of a huge range of puzzles for adults and children. For more information on our services, please visit us at www.pzle.co.uk. For information on purchasing puzzles for publication, visit us at www.clarity-media.co.uk

Puzzle Magazines

If you enjoy the puzzles in this book, then you may be interested in our puzzle magazines. We have a very large range of magazines that you can download and print yourself in PDF format at our Puzzle Magazine site. For more information, take a look at http://www.puzzle-magazine.com

Online Puzzles

If you prefer to play puzzles online, please take a look at the Puzzle Club website, at
www.thepuzzleclub.com

We also have more puzzle books available at www.puzzle-book.co.uk

Brain Game 1

Can you spot the three identical shapes? Shapes may be rotated and/or mirrored but will always be the same in size.

Brain Game 2

Can you find the matching key?

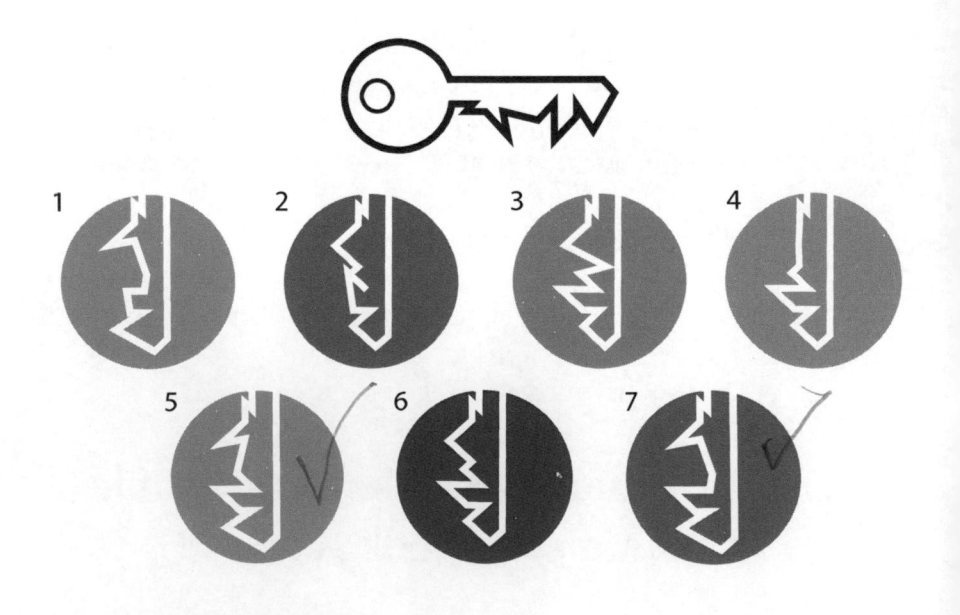

Find the words in the shaped grid. Words may be written horizontally, vertically or diagonally and in either a forwards or backwards direction.

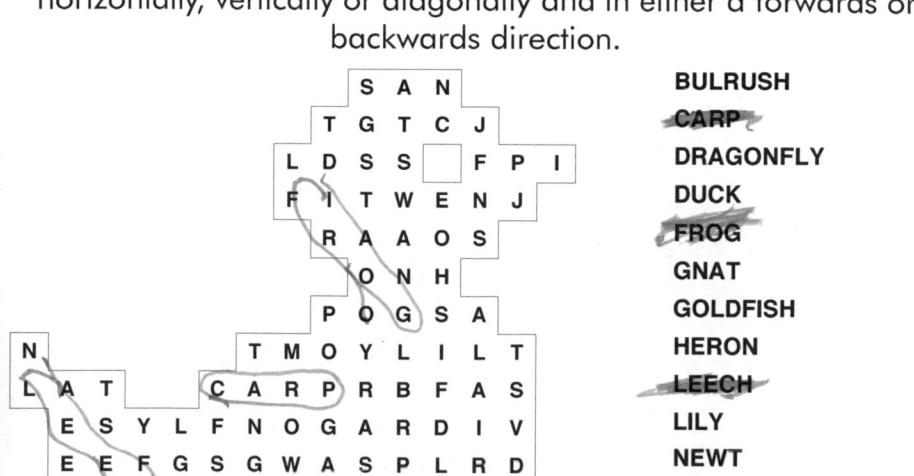

BULRUSH
CARP
DRAGONFLY
DUCK
FROG
GNAT
GOLDFISH
HERON
LEECH
LILY
NEWT
SNAIL
SWAN
TADPOLE
WORM

Brain Game 4

Follow the trail to see which kite the hand is holding.

Don't forget to take regular breaks between puzzles. Your brain is working hard!

Brain Game 5

Can you spot the 8 differences between the two pictures?

Brain Game 6

Which of A-D represents the reflection of the word in the box? The dashed-line represents the position of the mirror.

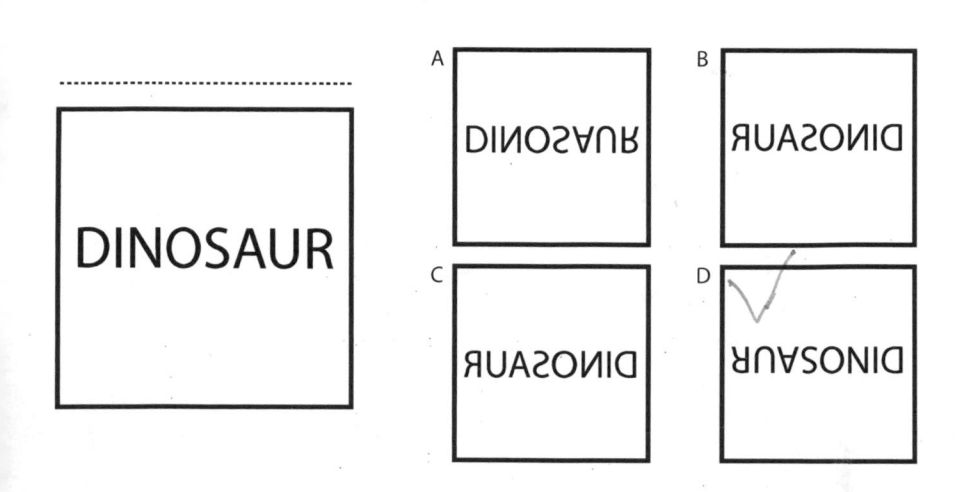

Brain Game 7

The value of each square in the number pyramid is the sum of the two squares directly under it.

247

140 137

73

37

16 15 21 16

13 3 12 9

It helps to start with the easier sums at the bottom of the pyramid and work upwards!

Brain Game 8

Using the colour key below, fill in the image to create a completed image.

Colour 1: Yellow   Colour 2: Red   Colour 3: Orange   Colour 4: Peach

					2	2																						2	2
		2	2	2	2																								2
	2	2	2	2																								2	2
2	1	1	2	2																							2	2	2
2	1	1	4	2	2						3	3															2	2	3
2	1	4	4	2	2						3	4	2	2									2	2	3	3			
1	2	4	4	2	2					3	3	2	3	2								2	3	3	4				
1	4	3	4	2	2					3	2	2	2							2	3	3	4	4					
1	4	4	3	2	2				3	3	2							2	2	3	4	4	3						
2	4	4	3	2	2				3	2	2						2	2	3	3	3	4	3						
1	1	3	3	3	2	2			3	3	2	2	2				2	2	3	3	4	1	4	3					
1	2	1	1	3	2	2	2		3	3	2	3	2	2		2	2	2	3	4	4	1	4	3					
1	1	4	1	4	3	2	2	2	2	2	2	2	2	4	2	2	2	2	2	2	4	4	3	4	4	4	4	3	
1	1	1	1	4	3	4	4	4	3	3	3	4	4	4	4	3	3	3	4	4	4	4	3	4	4	4	4	4	1
1	2	1	2	4	4	4	4	3	3	3	4	4	4	3	3	4	3	4	4	4	4	4	3	4	3	4	4	3	1
1	2	1	4	4	4	4	4	3	4	4	4	3	2	4	4	4	3	4	4	4	4	4	4	4	4	4	4	3	1
1	1	4	4	4	4	3	4	2	4	4	3	3	2	4	3	3	2	4	4	4	3	1	1	1	3	1	1	1	1
2	1	2	4	4	4	4	1	1	3	2	2	2	2	4	3	2	2	2	2	2	2	1	1	2	2	2	2	2	2
1	1	1	3	1	1	1	1	2	2	2	2	2	2	4	4	2	2	1	2	2	2	2	2	2	2	2	2	2	1
	2	2	1	3	2	2	2			2	2	4	2	2	1	1				2	2	2							
	2	2	2	2						2	2	2	1	1	3														
	2	2								3	3	3	1	3	3														
									2	1	1	1	1	3															
								3	1	1	1	3																	
							2	3	1	1	3																		
						2	3	1	3	3	3																		
					2	2	3	1	3	3																			
				2	3	3	1	1	3	3																			
	2	2	2	2	3	1	1	1	3	3																			
		3	3	3	1	1	3	3	3																				

Can you work out what this mythical creature is?

Find as many words of three or more letters in the wheel as you can. Each word must use the central letter and a selection from the outer wheel - no letter may be used more times than it appears in the wheel. Can you find the nine-letter word hidden in the wheel?

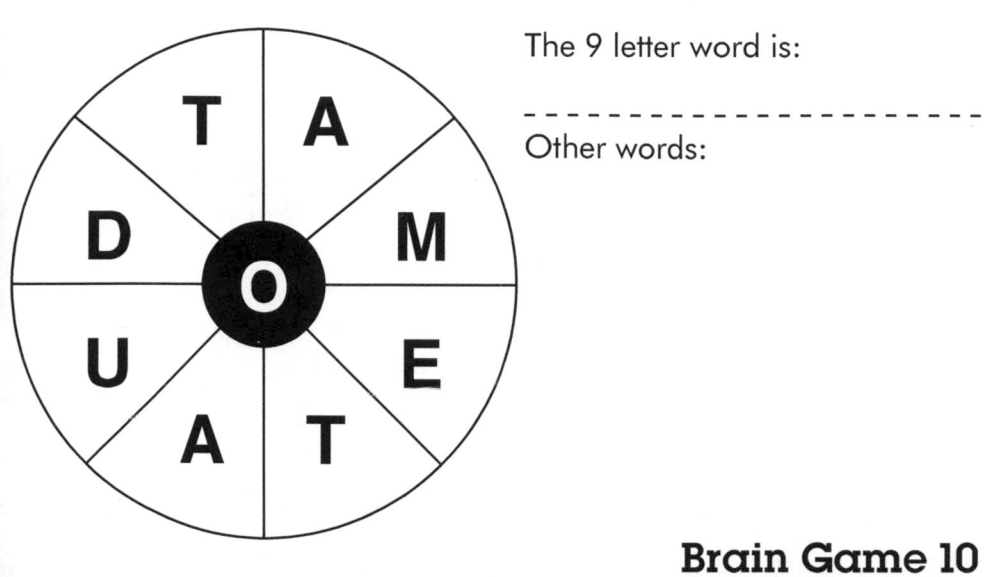

The 9 letter word is:

- -

Other words:

Draw a continuous line from START to END that goes through the maze without breaking through any walls.

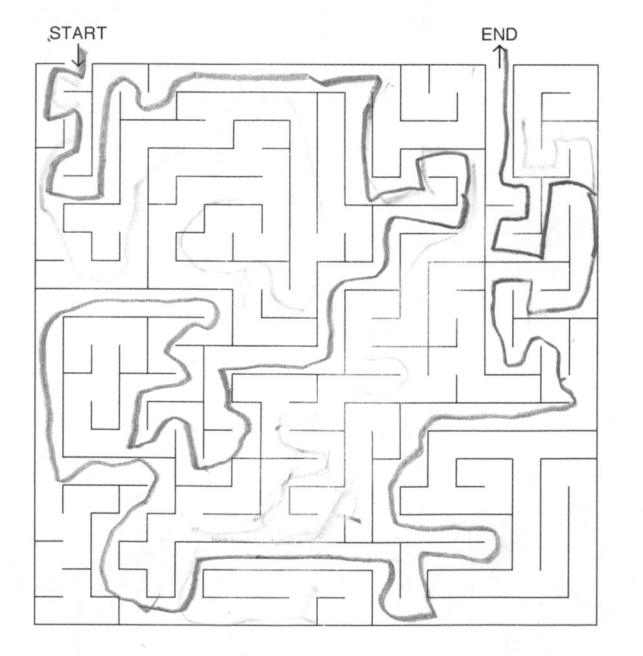

Brain Game 11

			4	1	5
					6
6		2			
			6		1
4					
2	6	3			

Place each number from 1-6 exactly once in each of the 6 horizontal rows and the 6 vertical columns. In addition each 2x3 bold-lined region of cells must contain the numbers from 1-6 exactly once.

Brain Game 12

Follow the path completing the sums as you go.

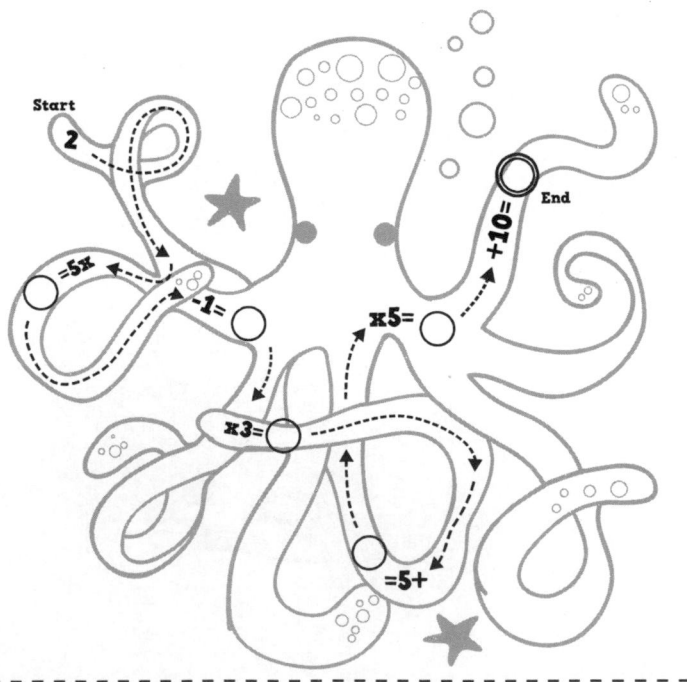

Can you connect the clock faces to the instructions and match the times up? The first one has been done for you.

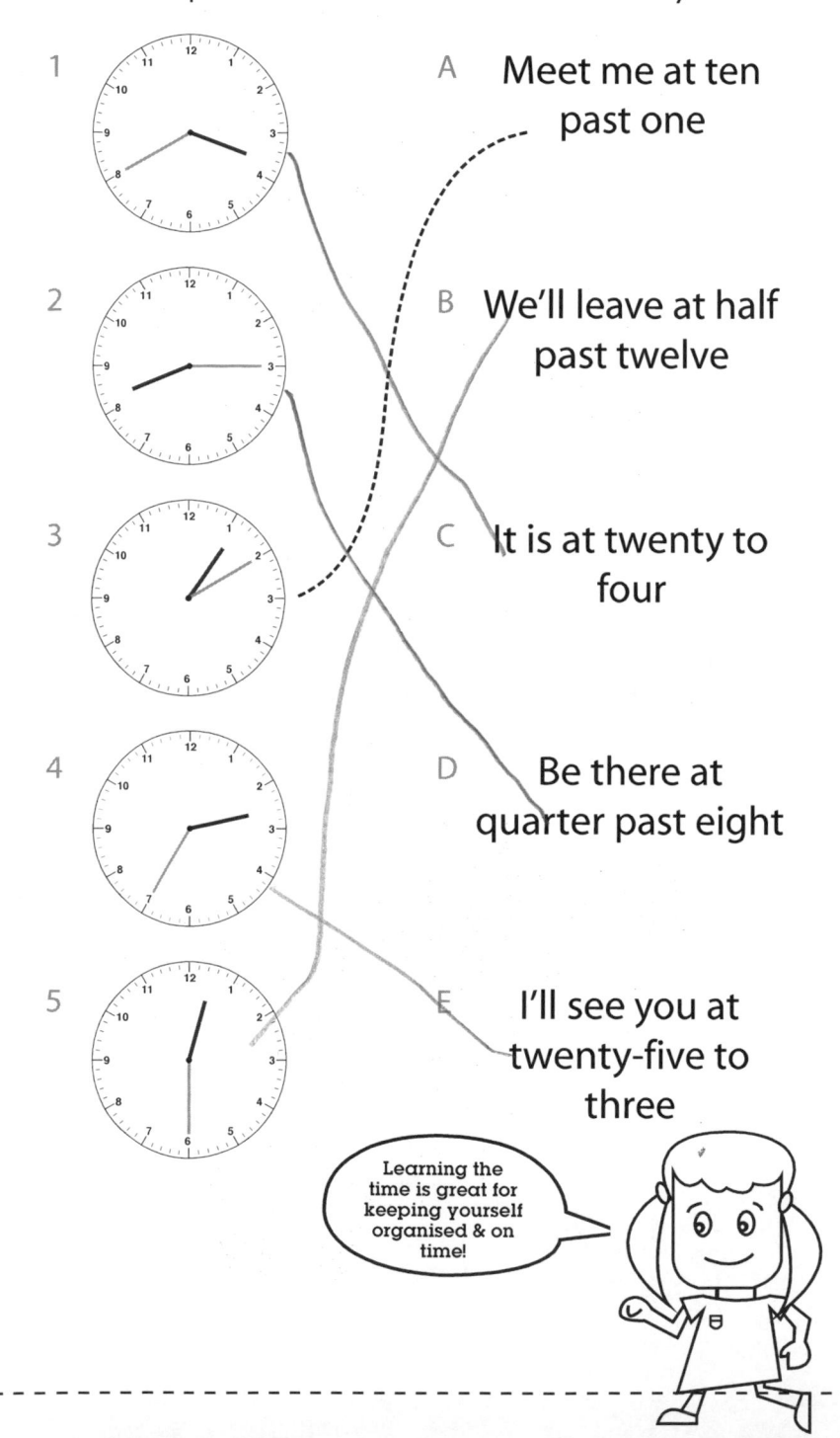

1

2

3

4

5

A Meet me at ten past one

B We'll leave at half past twelve

C It is at twenty to four

D Be there at quarter past eight

E I'll see you at twenty-five to three

Learning the time is great for keeping yourself organised & on time!

Brain Game 14

10 flowers are in a pile. Which one is at the bottom of the pile?

Brain Game 15

Can you work out the popular word/phrase illustrated by the image below?

Solve the clues to fill the crossword grid.

Across

1 - Flying machine (10)

5 - Go to see (5)

7 - Turn a wheel; guide a vehicle (5)

9 - Casual walk (6)

10 - Bite and munch food (4)

12 - Maths problems (4)

13 - Quick look (6)

16 - Make late; hold up (5)

17 - Birds lay their eggs in these (5)

18 - Exciting journeys (10)

Down

1 - Bees live in these (5)

2 - Large animals such as cows (6)

3 - Opposite of pull (4)

4 - Large animals with trunks (9)

6 - ___ eggs: tasty breakfast food (9)

8 - Uncooked (of food) (3)

11 - Eg Mars or Jupiter (6)

12 - Unhappy (3)

14 - Becomes less difficult (5)

15 - A rubber ring fitted around the wheel of a vehicle (4)

Brain Game 17

Moving from one letter to another, can you find a path that visits every square and spells each of the words listed under the puzzle? Start on the shaded square.

I	R	E	P	M	I	Y	L	D	N
O	D	I	N	G	C	R	E	D	E
U	N	E	V	I	N	H	E	I	I
S	E	P	I	P	P	A	L	B	R
P	R	N	S	I	E	S	T	R	F
P	E	E	T	N	I	T	A	E	Y
A	S	P	O	I	T	N	S	S	A
R	E	T	S	E	L	E	E	U	Q
N	L	A	R	N	S	E	L	E	I
O	C	T	U	A	L	T	T	D	P

Assayer, Entitle, Friendly, Happiest, Imperious, Incredible, Intensive, Nocturnal, Pending, Pique, Postal, Prepares, Settled

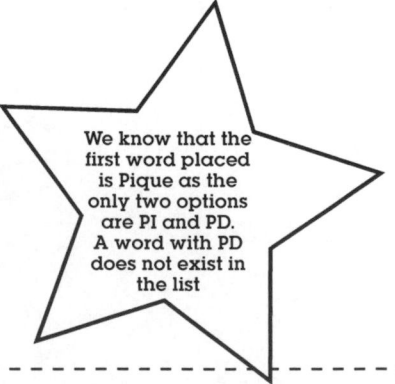

We know that the first word placed is Pique as the only two options are PI and PD. A word with PD does not exist in the list

Circle the coins below to show how much money you will need to buy the sweets, and then work out how much you have left!

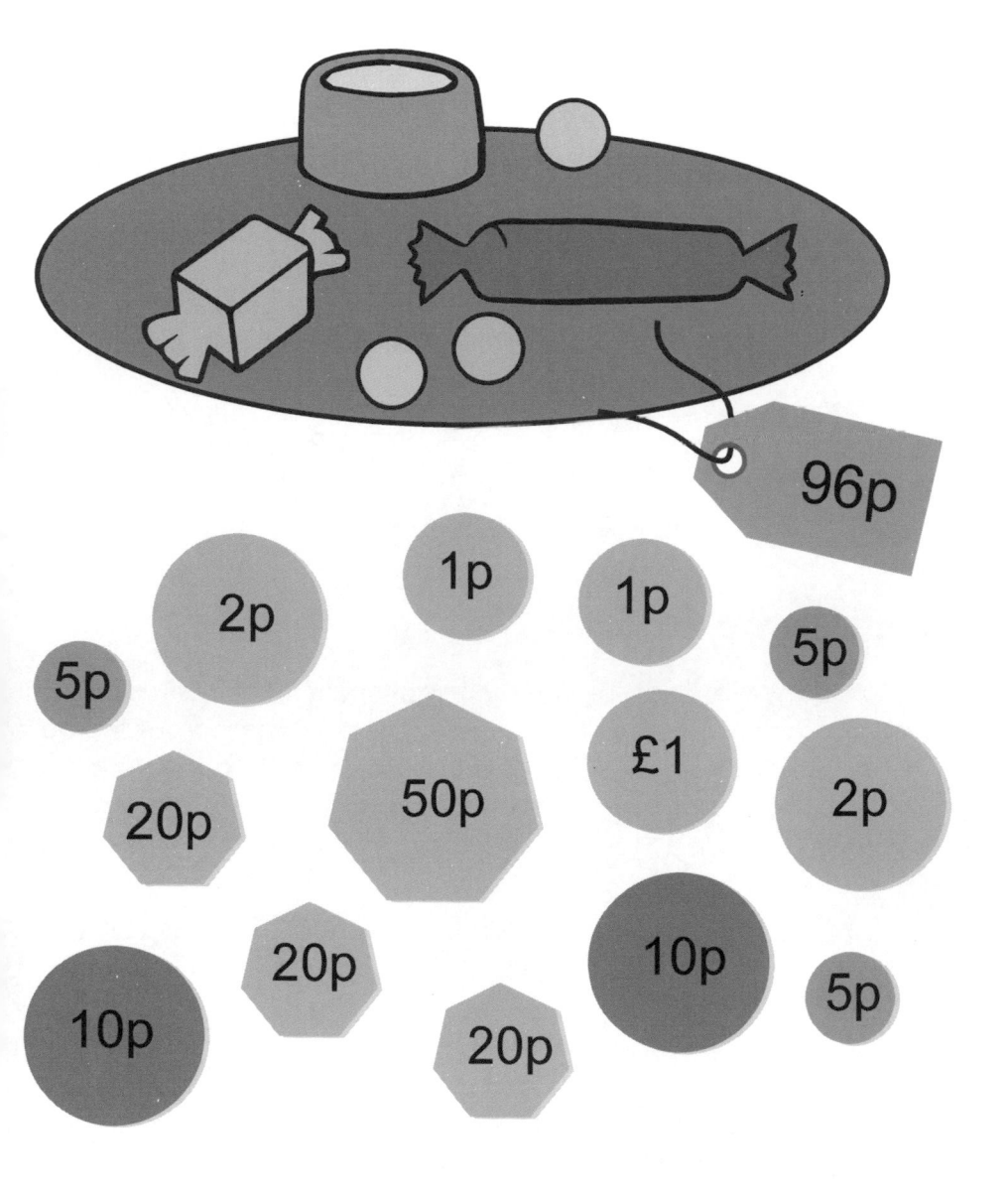

96p

2p

1p

1p

5p

5p

20p

50p

£1

2p

20p

10p

5p

10p

20p

How much do you have left? _____

Brain Game 19

		22	15
	21		11
	20		14
	8		

Complete the magic square so that the total of the numbers in each row, column and the two diagonals is **58**.

Each number from **7-22** appears once in the grid.

Brain Game 20

Find as many words of three or more letters in the wheel as you can. Each word must use the central letter and a selection from the outer wheel - no letter may be used more times than it appears in the wheel. Can you find the nine-letter word hidden in the wheel?

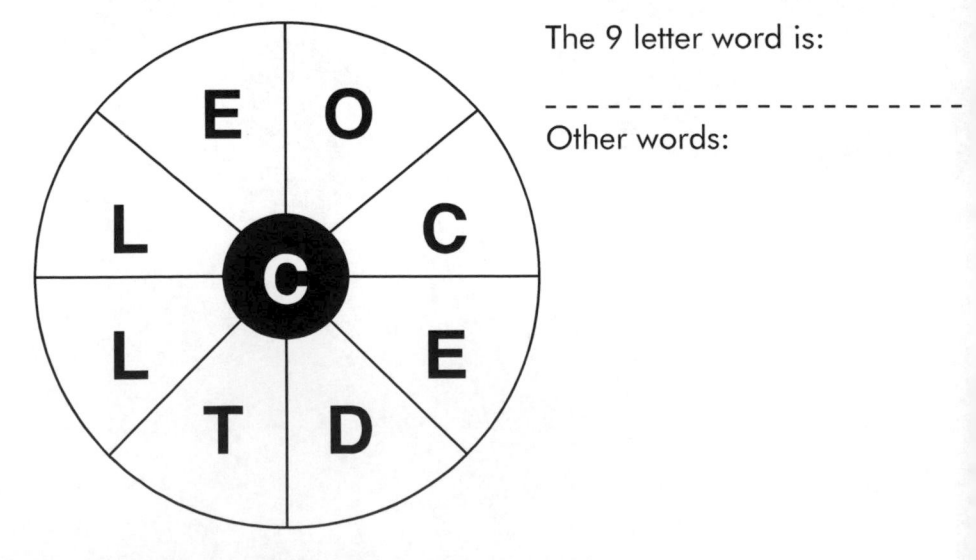

The 9 letter word is:

- - - - - - - - - - - - - - - - -

Other words:

Follow the paths to create an anagram of the top word.

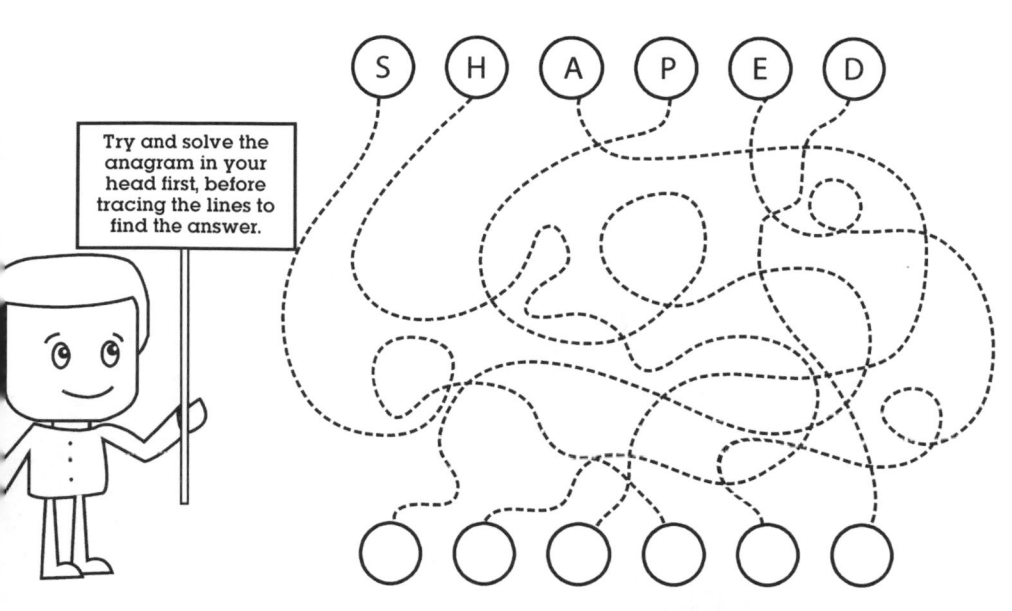

Try and solve the anagram in your head first, before tracing the lines to find the answer.

S H A P E D

Can you see which picture exactly matches the silhouette?

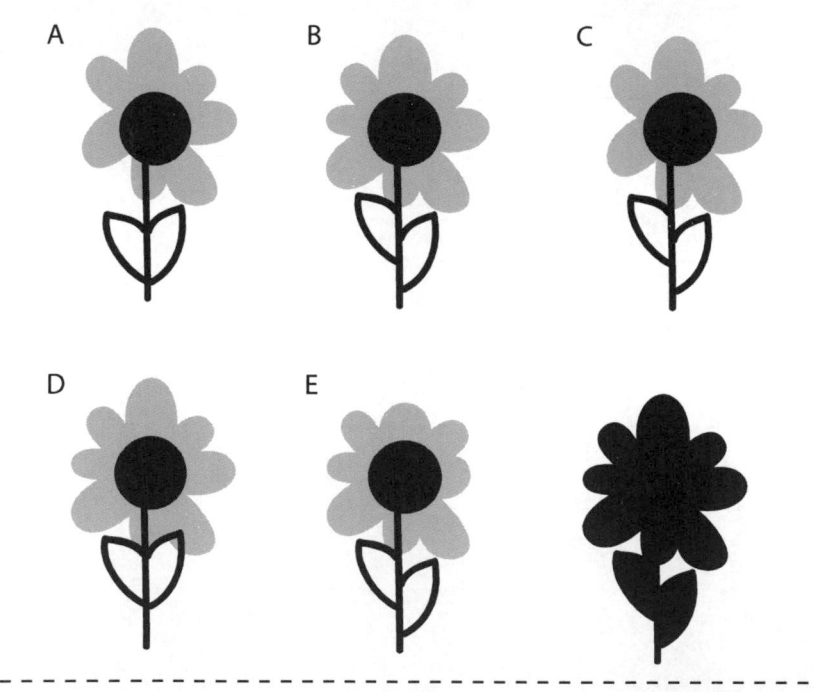

A   B   C

D   E

Brain Game 23

3				4	
	6			3	
1		6			
			6		4
	5			2	
	2				3

Place each number from 1-6 exactly once in each of the 6 horizontal rows and the 6 vertical columns. In addition each 2x3 bold-lined region of cells must contain the numbers from 1-6 exactly once.

Brain Game 24

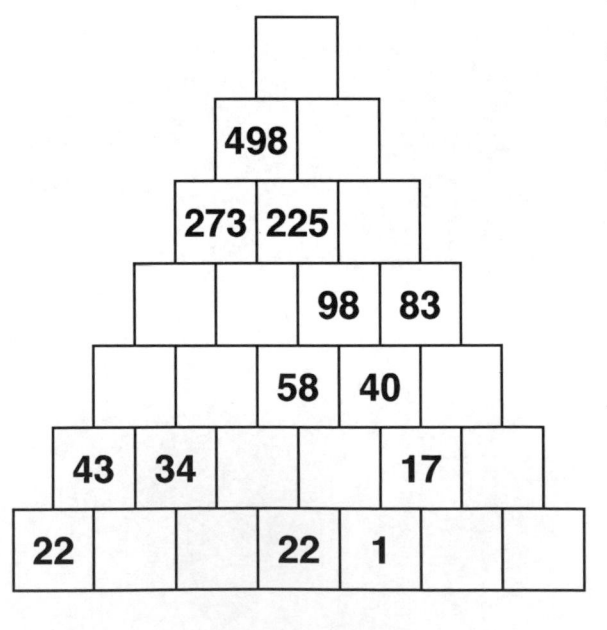

The value of each square in the number pyramid is the sum of the two squares directly under it.

Connect all dots from number 1 onwards.

Once you have connected the dots, why not colour the image in?

Brain Game 26

When the shape is rotated 90° left, will it look like A, B, C or D?

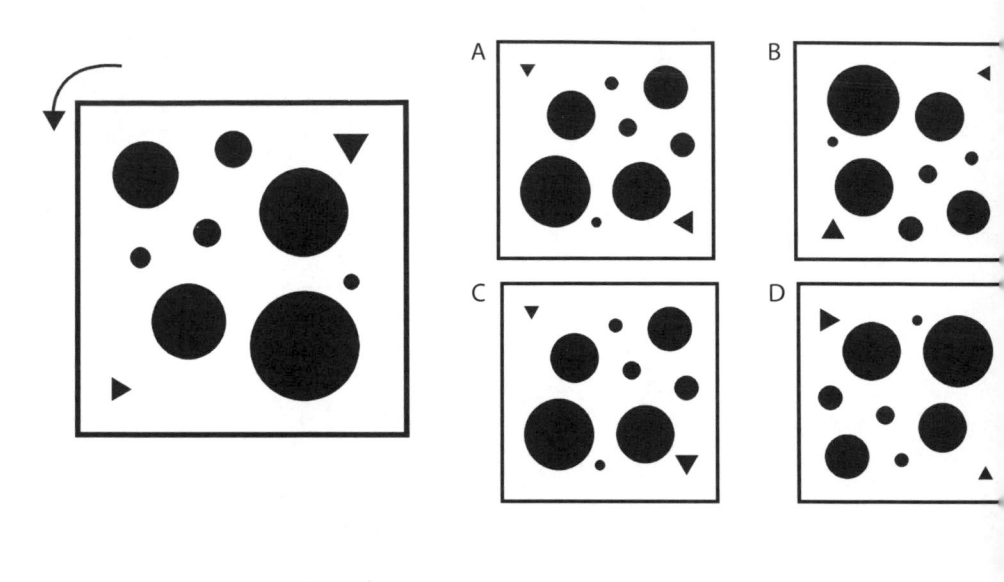

Brain Game 27

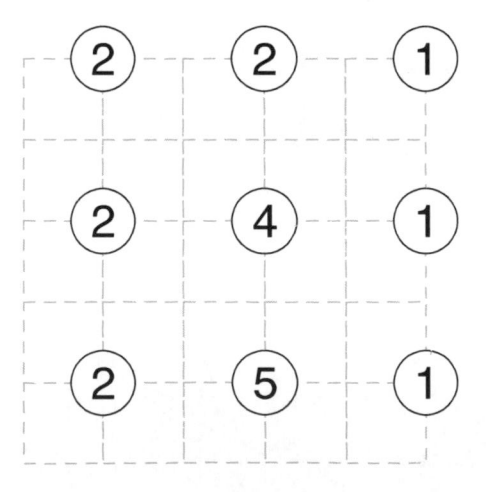

Connect every island (represented by circles) into a single interconnected group. To do this draw bridges between islands. The number in each circle states how many bridges must be connected to that island. Bridges cannot cross each other, can only be drawn horizontally or vertically, and there can be a maximum of two bridges between any pair of islands.

Brain Game 28

Shade in the numbers that are divisible by 5. Once complete, you will reveal a 'fishy' image!

82	27	8	26	55	90	75	20	5	1	8	32	16	7	27	42	62	14	80	15
11	16	19	45	5	25	65	80	95	95	85	32	64	68	9	80	85	55	30	80
64	78	95	55	55	90	85	70	15	65	70	5	1	45	45	80	85	70	35	92
72	39	90	45	55	25	95	20	40	20	10	65	35	15	10	35	15	80	85	82
39	35	75	85	90	80	60	10	40	80	85	40	45	50	70	80	15	70	45	63
23	70	50	30	50	95	95	70	60	5	5	45	25	15	55	35	95	5	88	43
34	95	45	20	60	15	50	50	80	30	40	20	15	85	5	20	10	95	67	91
10	10	80	75	19	38	66	93	85	60	35	90	20	30	40	80	30	55	8	86
5	5	62	54	66	77	93	73	90	55	55	65	90	20	10	65	10	55	54	54
81	18	61	41	23	86	48	53	5	80	32	5	85	95	95	40	30	5	92	37
52	22	77	9	48	64	71	63	95	50	1	81	95	65	60	15	10	35	19	38
31	69	89	58	58	55	33	33	17	55	38	14	41	90	20	85	15	40	47	93
4	74	7	32	31	20	35	73	29	61	5	53	53	90	15	25	60	85	39	53
27	23	93	69	92	25	70	89	24	57	23	46	8	73	70	20	15	55	1	26
38	17	92	27	40	55	70	32	84	72	88	6	32	8	80	20	95	30	71	36
7	32	89	79	50	15	90	83	28	74	48	29	87	13	90	50	60	68	89	8
53	52	5	70	15	45	5	29	18	33	49	84	9	4	65	90	45	11	49	64
43	10	65	40	45	85	90	40	34	72	88	14	62	90	60	40	65	1	26	6
69	84	83	86	11	50	95	60	15	25	25	90	25	35	70	65	19	9	14	94
59	62	63	17	23	42	60	45	20	95	10	15	70	60	13	79	74	73	79	51

Brain Game 29

Can you find the matching key?

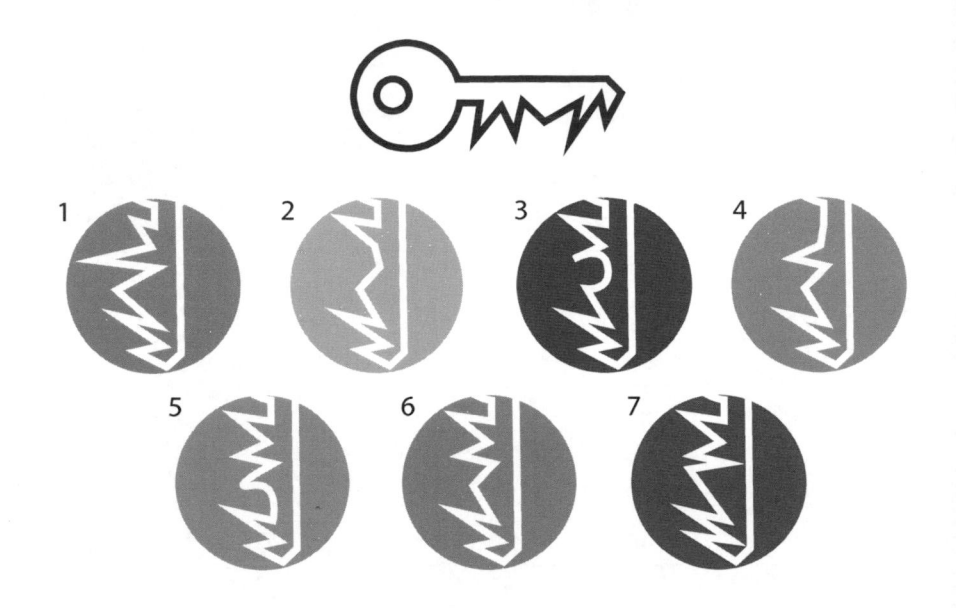

Brain Game 30

Enter the numbers from 1 - 9 once each into the puzzle grid, so as to complete the maths sums that read across and down the puzzle grid. Perform sums from left to right and top to bottom.

Fill the grid with the number sequences given in the list. A few have been placed to start you off.

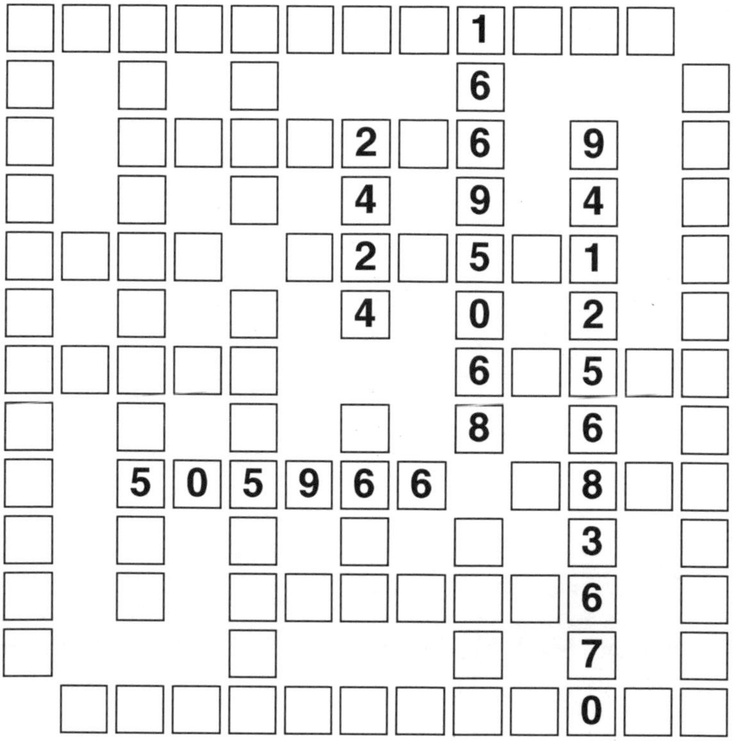

4 numbers
1364
~~2424~~
3935
5585
8657
8885

5 numbers
56689
60500

6 numbers
~~505966~~
821541

7 numbers
1731286
2975366

8 numbers
~~16695068~~
99756222

11 numbers
87168560574
~~94125683670~~

12 numbers
106410959260
260353534972
298435321789
890214143010

Brain Game 32

		1		3	
				2	1
2					4
3					2
1	5				
	4		5		

Place each number from 1-6 exactly once in each of the 6 horizontal rows and the 6 vertical columns. In addition each 2x3 bold-lined region of cells must contain the numbers from 1-6 exactly once.

Brain Game 33

Find the words in the shaped grid. Words may be written horizontally, vertically or diagonally and in either a forwards or backwards direction.

```
            F  T  R  Z  I
         S  P  U  E
      E  U  I  U  R  T              T
      P  Z  O  L  T  A              S
   S  S  L  E  S  L  W  T  S     R  A
   H  T  U  F  R  E  T  S  B  O  L  O
X  A  V  I     B  K  L  E  H  W  C  A
I  R  I  B  N  •  P  L  A  N  K  T  O  N
K  B  A  N  G  E  L  F  I  S  H  O  A  M  C
W  L  A  R  O  C  K  E  L  P  L  D  M  H
   S  C  A  L  L  O  P  U  O  E  E     O
   B  Y  E  A  E  S  O  A  I  D     R
      E  N  O  M  E  N  A
         L  U  O  T
         Q  J  T  U
```

ANCHOR
ANEMONE
ANGELFISH
CORAL
EEL
KELP
LOBSTER
OCTOPUS
PLANKTON
SALT WATER
SCALLOP
SHARK
STINGRAY
TURTLE
WHELK

Can you guess the words written on the folded paper?

CELEBRATION

HOLIDAYS

Complete the grid so that each row and column contains three 0s and three 1s. The same number cannot appear in more than two consecutive squares in any row or column. In the finished puzzle, each row must have a different sequence of 0s and 1s to any other row, and likewise for each column.

		1	1		
1		1	1		
1	1				
				1	
					0

Brain Game 36

Can you find the 3 matching pairs of turtles?

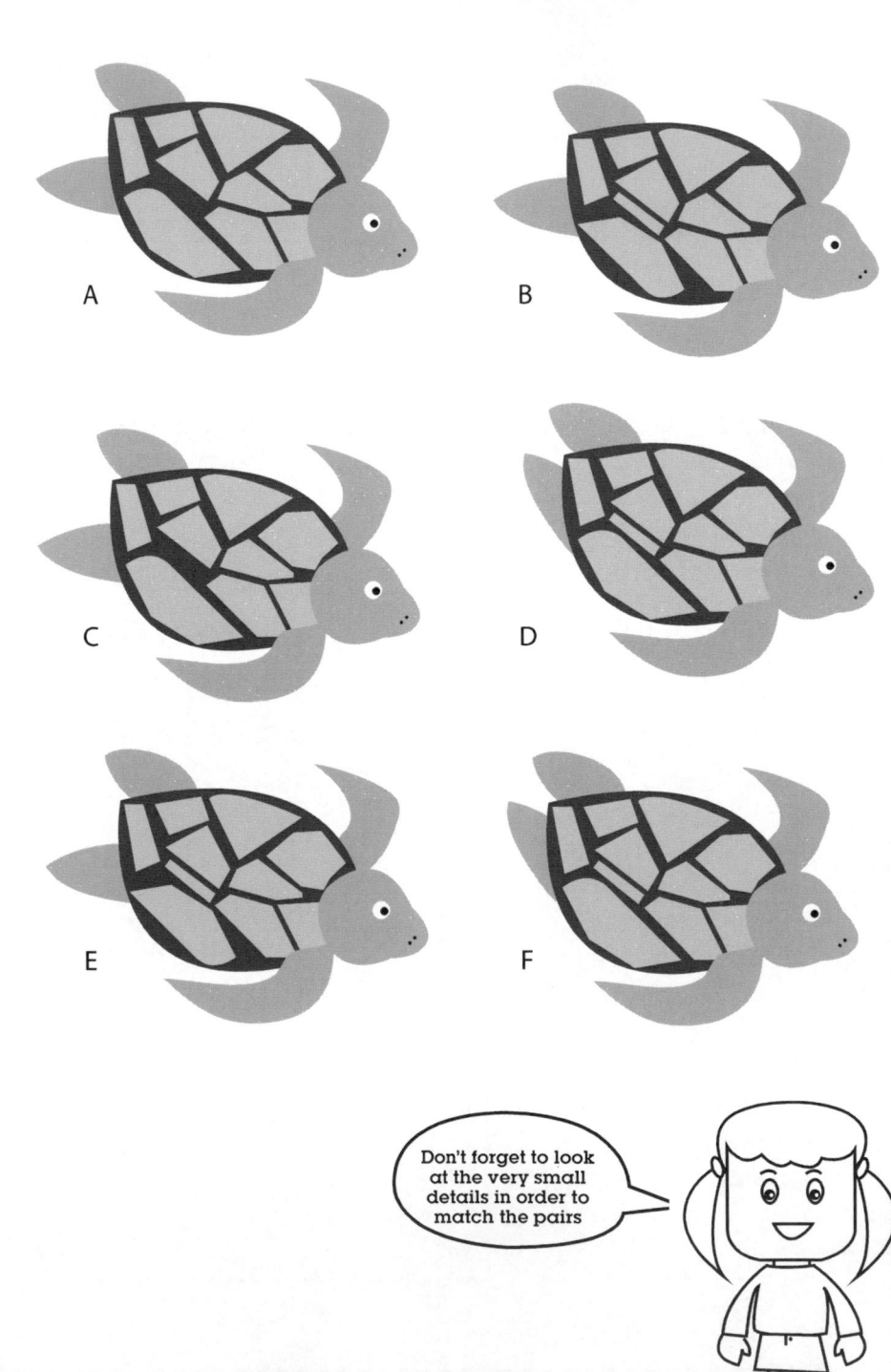

Don't forget to look at the very small details in order to match the pairs

Follow the path completing the sums as you go.

Answer the clues to the right of each row. The answers will read the same horizontally and vertically.

Move downwards (in water)

Metal

You breathe through this

Leg joint

Brain Game 39

Using the colour key below, fill in the image to create a completed image.

Colour 1: Purple   Colour 2: Pink

1	1				2	2							2	2				1	1
1	1	1				2	2	2			2	2	2				1	1	1
1	1	1	1	1			2				2				1	1	1	1	1
1	1	1	1	1	1	1			2	2			1	1	1	1	1	1	1
1	1	2	2	1	1	1	1		2	2		1	1	1	1	2	2	1	1
1	1	2	2	1	1	1	1	1	1	1	1	1	1	1	1	2	2	1	1
	1	1	1	1	1	1	1	1	1	1	1	1	1	1	1	1	1	1	
	1	1	1	1	2	2	1	1	1	1	1	1	2	2	1	1	1	1	
	1	1	1	1	2	2	1	1	1	1	1	1	2	2	1	1	1	1	
		1	1	1	1	1	1	1	1	1	1	1	1	1	1	1	1		
				1	1	1	1	1	1	1	1	1	1	1	1				
						1	1	2	2	1	1	2	2	1	1				
				1	1	2	2	2	1	1	2	2	2	1	1				
			1	2	2	2	2	2	1	1	2	2	2	2	2	1			
		1	2	2	2	2	2	2	1	1	2	2	2	2	2	2	1		
	1	1	2	2	2	2	1	1	1	1	1	1	2	2	2	2	1	1	
	1	2	2	2	1	1	1					1	1	1	2	2	2	1	
1	1	1	1	1											1	1	1	1	1
1	1																	1	1

A number or letter has been split in to four and the pieces have been swapped and rotated. Can you guess what it is?

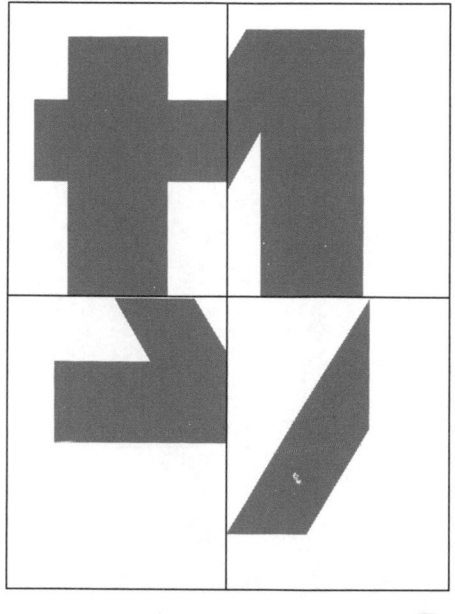

Can you work out the next letter in the sequence below?

CYWOTNLITS_

Clue- the answer is right here on this page!

Brain Game 42

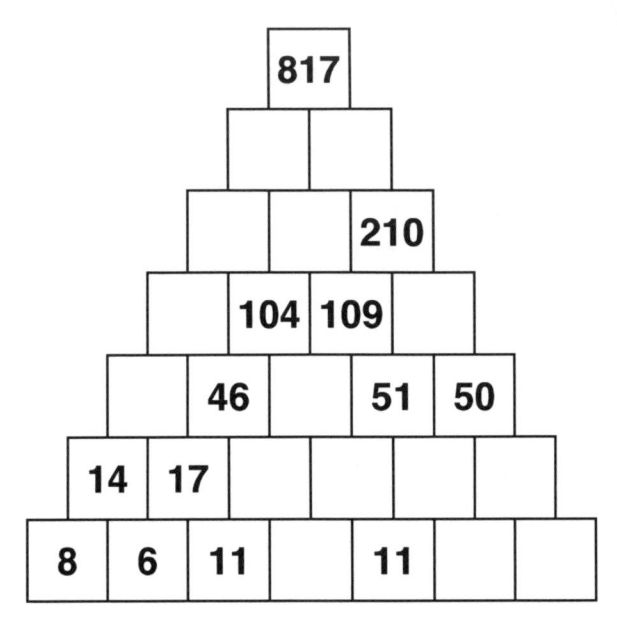

The value of each square in the number pyramid is the sum of the two squares directly under it.

Brain Game 43

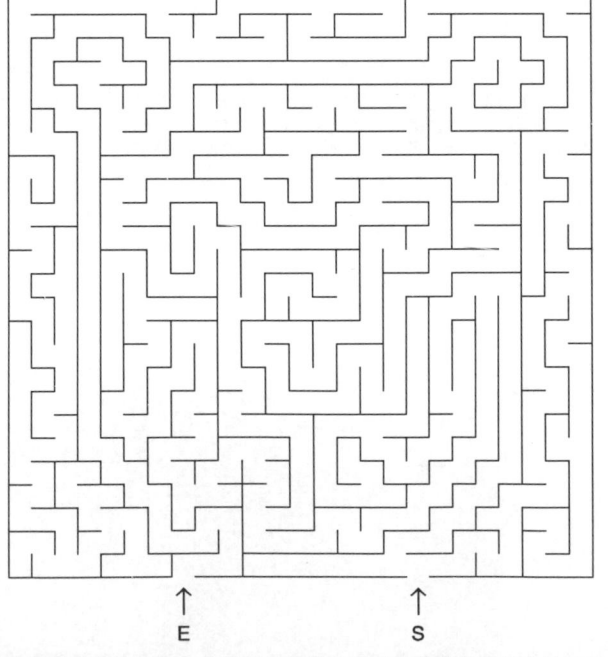

Draw a continuous line from START to END that goes through the maze without breaking through any walls. Once complete, can you work out what the animal is?

Brain Game 44

		13	
9	21	10	
	12		15
23			

Complete the magic square so that the total of the numbers in each row, column and the two diagonals is 62.

Each number from 8-23 appears once in the grid.

Brain Game 45

Cross out any letter that occurs more than once in the grid to reveal a hidden word.

S	E	T	Z	U
E	P	R	C	D
I	E	O	D	U
T	Z	N	W	W
O	D	C	G	T

Brain Game 46

Find as many words of three or more letters in the wheel as you can. Each word must use the central letter and a selection from the outer wheel - no letter may be used more times than it appears in the wheel. Can you find the nine-letter word hidden in the wheel?

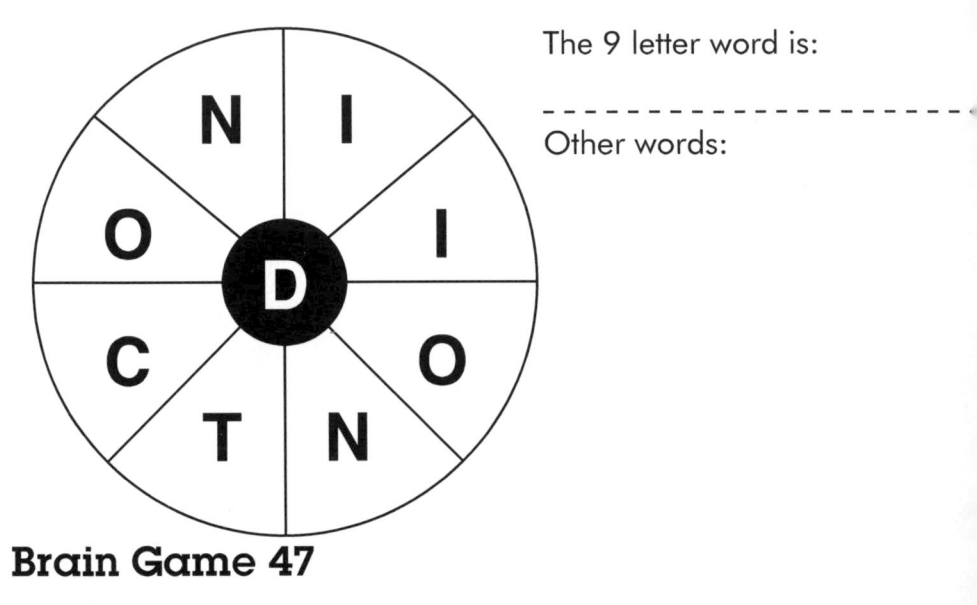

The 9 letter word is:

- - - - - - - - - - - - - - - - - - - -

Other words:

Brain Game 47

Can you work out the popular word/phrase illustrated by the image below?

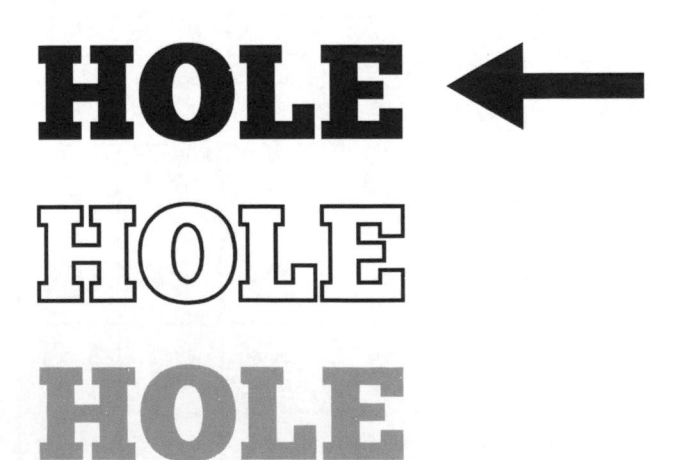

- -

Brain Game 48

Fill the grid with the number sequences given in the list. A few have been placed to start you off.

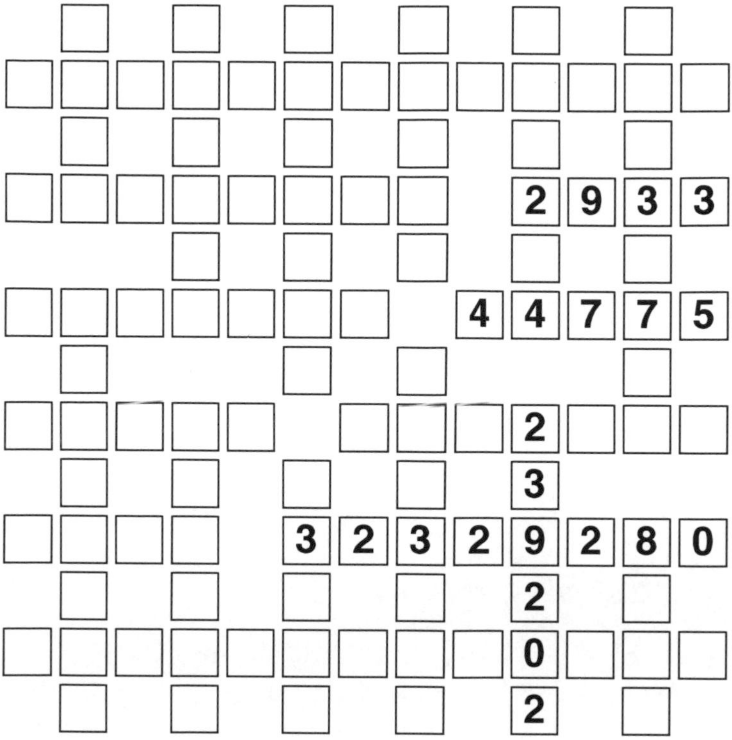

4 numbers
2206
~~2933~~
3334
8460

5 numbers
13955
43880
~~44775~~
55859

6 numbers
~~239202~~
590702
596274
816087

7 numbers
1002184
1342190
2547892
7043788

8 numbers
31302194
~~32329280~~
94475715
94634718

13 numbers
4948955890264
7359156569545

Brain Game 49

Draw a continuous line from START to END that goes through the maze without breaking through any walls.

Brain Game 50

A number or letter has been split in to four and the pieces have been swapped and rotated. Can you guess what it is?

Can you guess the words written on the folded paper?

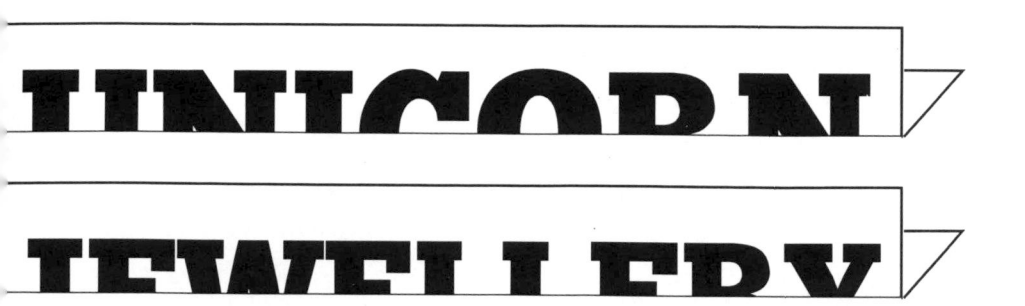

UNICORN

JEWELLERY

ORCHESTRA

Can you work out the cheery word that is revealed by this riddle?

My first is in SUN and in SHINE
My second's not in YOURS but is in MINE
My third's the middle letter of STICK
My fourth's not in PUSH but is in FLICK
My fifth's in EAT and in DINE.

Brain Game 53

4		2			
					6
		3	6		
		5	4		
1					
			3		4

Place each number from 1-6 exactly once in each of the 6 horizontal rows and the 6 vertical columns. In addition each 2x3 bold-lined region of cells must contain the numbers from 1-6 exactly once.

Brain Game 54

19		11		17	
			1		29
7			34		
32					13
36	25	22	5		27

A chess knight visits each square of the grid exactly once, starting at 1 and ending at 36. Deduce the whole path of the knight - some of which is already given - and thus complete the grid. The knight moves either two squares horizontally followed by one square vertically, or two squares vertically followed by one square horizontally.

Circle the coins below to show how much money you will need to buy the clothes, and then work out how much you have left!

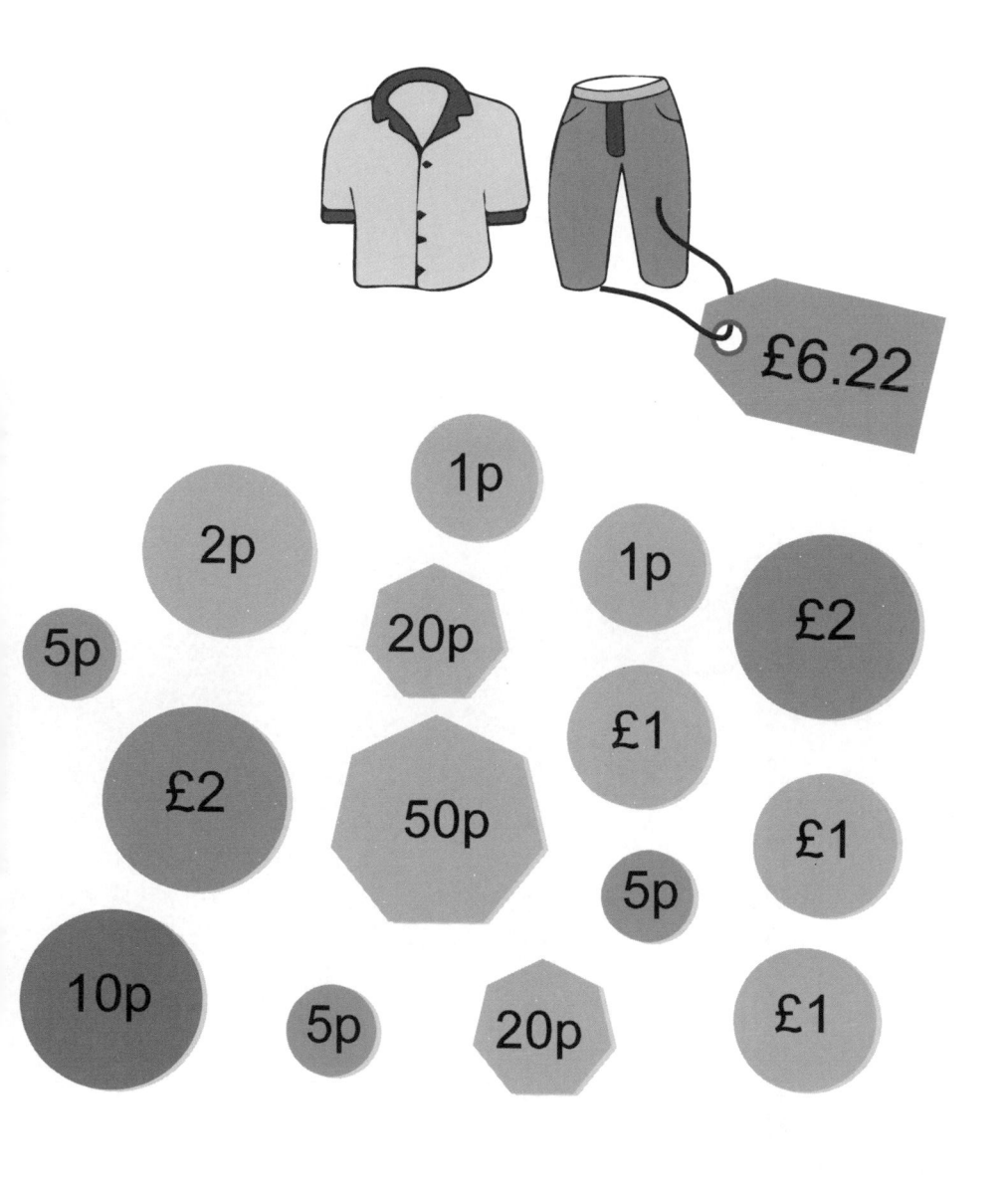

£6.22

1p

2p

5p

1p

20p

£2

£2

£1

50p

£1

5p

10p

5p

20p

£1

How much do you have left? _____

Brain Game 56

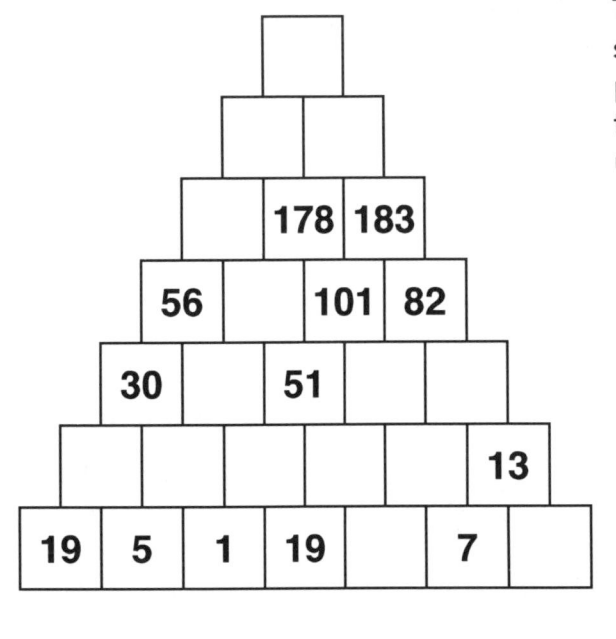

The value of each square in the number pyramid is the sum of the two squares directly under it.

Brain Game 57

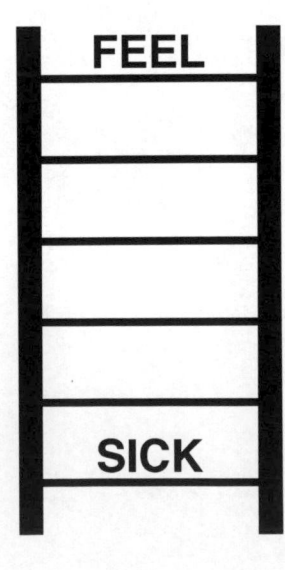

Move from the word at the top of the ladder to the word at the bottom of the ladder by changing one letter on each step of the ladder to make a valid word. Do not rearrange the order of the letters. There may be more than one way of doing this.

Each number represents a different letter of the alphabet. In this puzzle, the 13 represents a T for example. Complete the grid by working out what the other numbers represent.

23	6	13	14	13	6		22		11		26	
1		25			26	14	1	24	10	13	7	5
18	25	23			26		3		14		5	
18		13	6	15	7	8	22		16	14	25	8
8		6			5		25		24		4	
7	9	7	11	13		14	26	20	25	5	7	22
			6		3		21		16			
17	1	25	16	13	7	13		6	24	5	7	22
	16		19		16		11			6		1
23	25	7	5		7	12	6	13	25	11		26
	13		6		19		20			2	25	26
20	7	14	16	13	25	20	7			7		7
	26		13		13		13	14	5	13	14	16

A B C D E F G H I J K L M N O P Q R S T U V W X Y Z

1	2	3	4	5	6	7	8	9	10	11	12	13
		B		**R**			**L**		**H**	**C**		**T**

14	15	16	17	18	19	20	21	22	23	24	25	26
W	**N**											

Brain Game 59

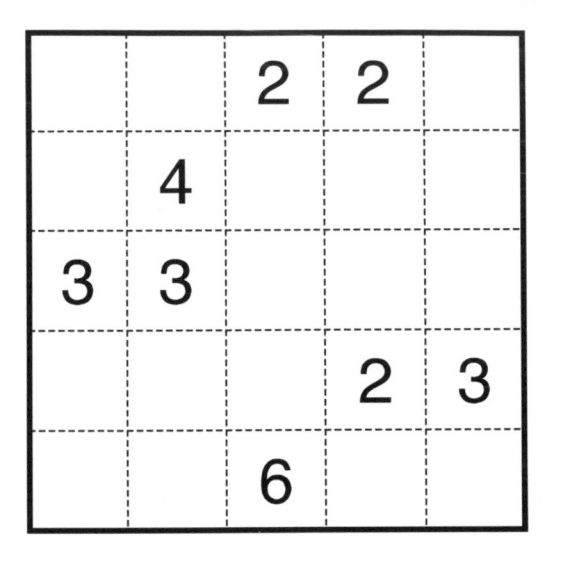

The grid contains blank squares and numbered squares. A numbered square must belong to a single rectangle containing the number of stated squares. There is only one numbered square in each rectangle.

Brain Game 60

Follow the path completing the sums as you go.

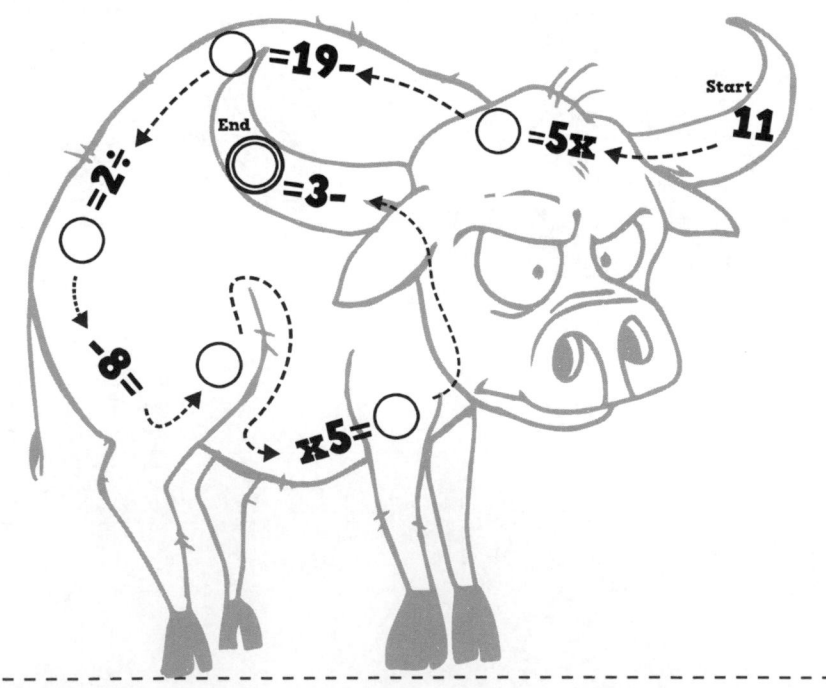

Brain Game 61

Fill the grid with the number sequences given in the list. A few have been placed to start you off.

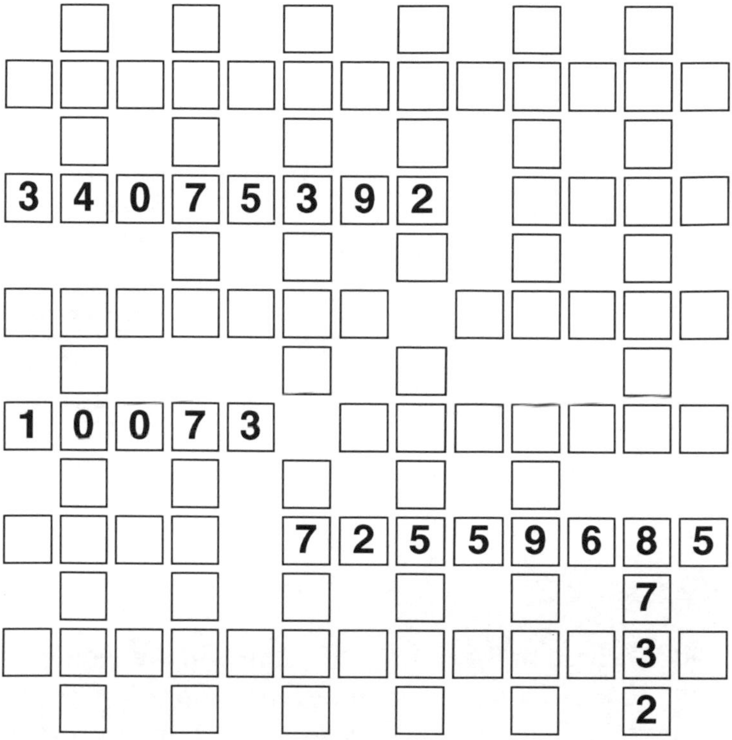

4 numbers
1034
7582
7955
~~8732~~

5 numbers
~~10073~~
57388
63804
77520

6 numbers
290773
467794
689982
742789

7 numbers
3866938
4324967
6875694
7643466

8 numbers
16252023
~~34075392~~
36065544
~~72559685~~

13 numbers
6096160749366
6448580988937

Brain Game 62

Find the words in the shaped grid. Words may be written horizontally, vertically or diagonally and in either a forwards or backwards direction.

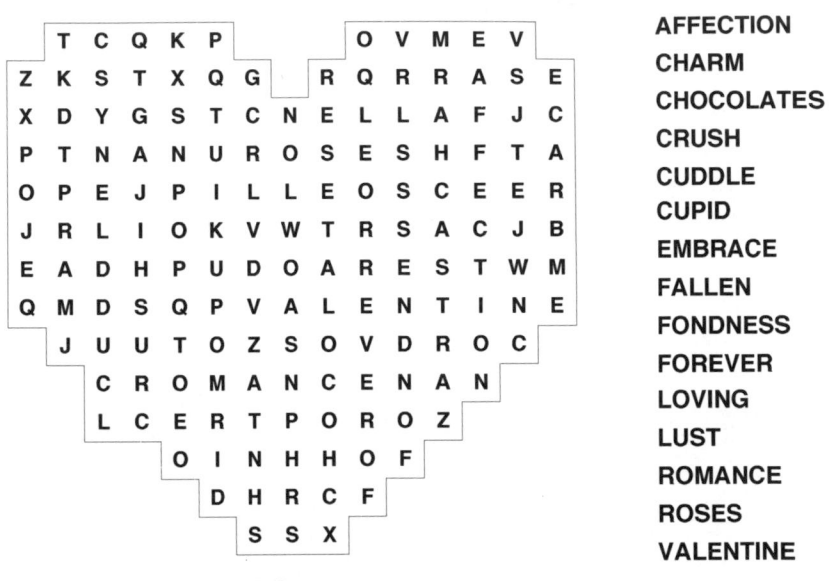

AFFECTION
CHARM
CHOCOLATES
CRUSH
CUDDLE
CUPID
EMBRACE
FALLEN
FONDNESS
FOREVER
LOVING
LUST
ROMANCE
ROSES
VALENTINE

Brain Game 63

Find as many words of three or more letters in the wheel as you can Each word must use the central letter and a selection from the outer wheel - no letter may be used more times than it appears in the wheel. Can you find the nine-letter word hidden in the wheel?

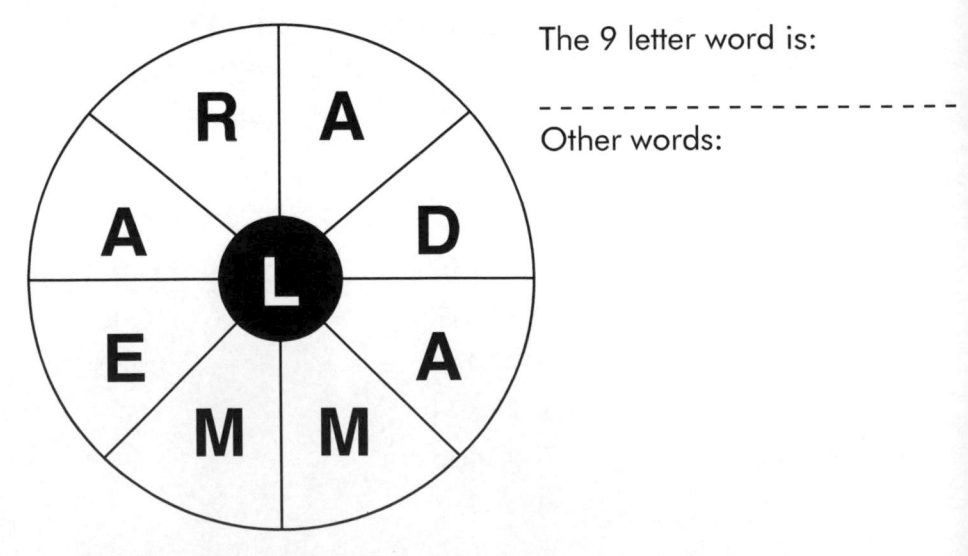

The 9 letter word is:

- -

Other words:

Connect all dots from number 1 onwards.

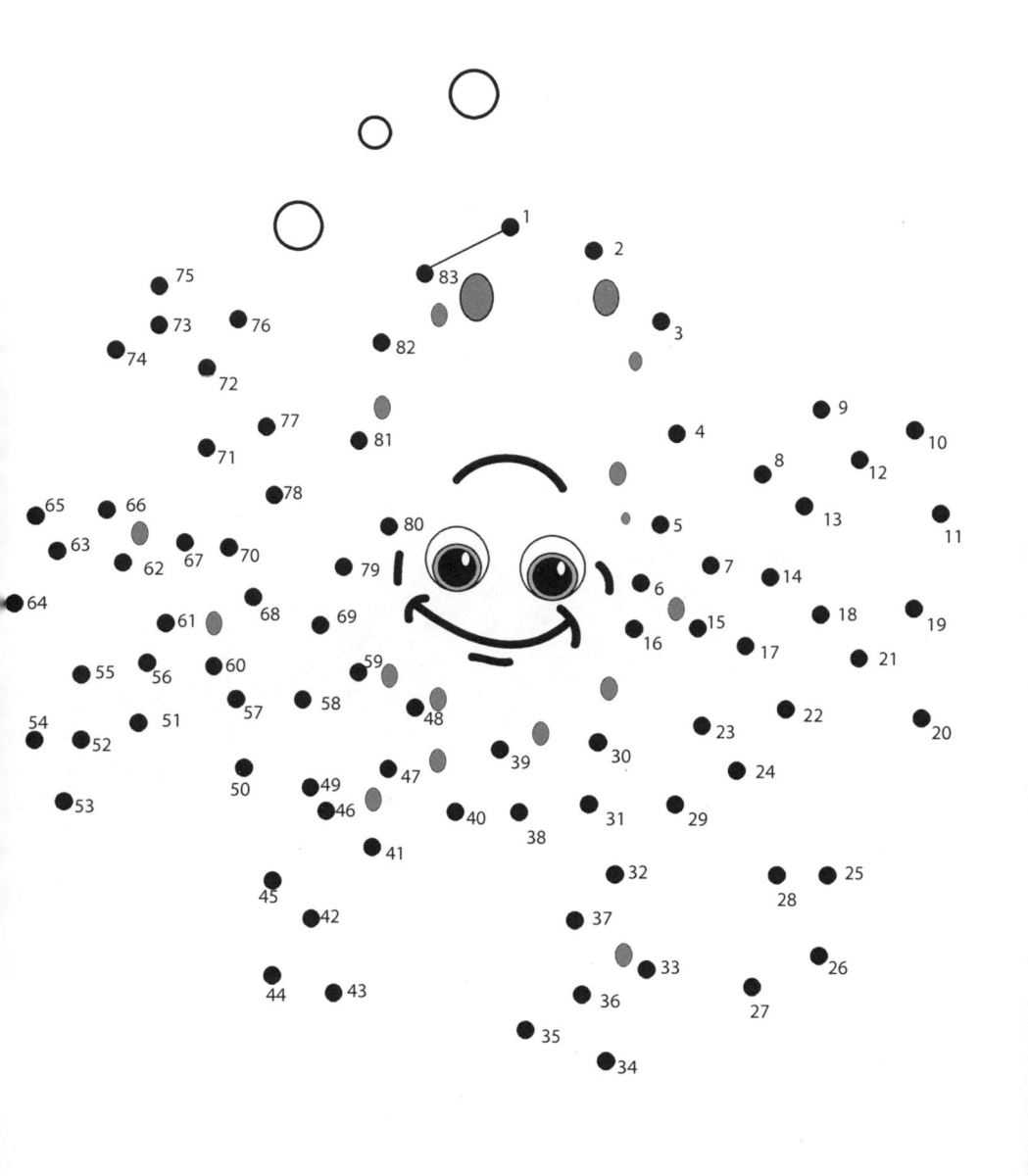

Brain Game 65

On this pair of scales you can see that two circles weigh the same as four squares. If a triangle is twice as heavy as a circle, can you work out how many squares would be required to balance three triangles?

Brain Game 66

17		12	5
		15	18
7			
			8

Complete the magic square so that the total of the numbers in each row, column and the two diagonals is 50.

Each number from 5-20 appears once in the grid.

Follow the paths to create an anagram of the top word. Can you solve it in your head first?

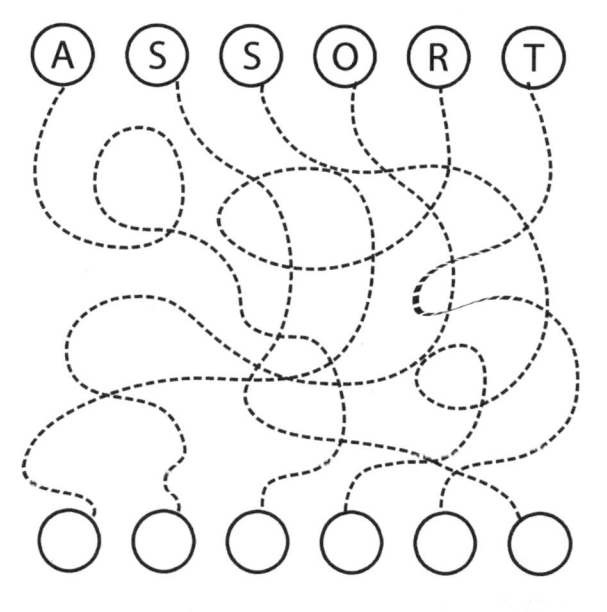

(A) (S) (S) (O) (R) (T)

Answer the clues to the right of each row. The answers will read the same horizontally and vertically.

Cook

Raised area of land

Otherwise

Run away

Brain Game 69

In this number crossword, fill the white squares so that the sum total of each across or down run of squares matches the total at the start of that run. A number cannot repeat within a run, and you must use numbers from 1-9 only.

Brain Game 70

2	+		÷		1
x		+		x	
	x		-		30
÷		x		+	
	-	1	-		0
1		12		37	

Enter the numbers from 1 - 9 once each into the puzzle grid, so as to complete the maths sums that read across and down the puzzle grid. Perform sums from left to right and top to bottom.

Each number represents a different letter of the alphabet. In this puzzle, the 14 represents a C for example. Complete the grid by working out what the other numbers represent.

24	17	17	6	19	12	■	5	■	6	■	12	■
1	■	9	■	11	1	14	2	19	12	14	1	
12	16	7	■	21	■	17	■	12	■	4	■	
26	■	22	4	12	5	14	17	■	7	4	10	25
1	■	4	■	7	■	7	■	22	■	4	■	
11	17	7	1	5	■	16	1	13	17	4	14	1
■	■	11	■	20	■	16	■	16	■	■	■	
23	1	11	7	4	17	11	■	12	23	12	18	1
■	10	■	16	■	9	■	16	■	20	■	15	
10	4	26	12	■	3	9	12	26	1	16	■	4
■	7	■	11	■	9	■	26	■	17	8	19	
14	17	11	14	16	1	7	1	■	12	■	1	
■	16	■	1	■	7	■	11	1	1	10	1	10

A B C D E F G H I J K L M N O P Q R S T U V W X Y Z

1	2	3	4	5	6	7	8	9	10	11	12	13
					P		W		D			

14	15	16	17	18	19	20	21	22	23	24	25	26
C	X				L		G				Y	

Brain Game 72

Find the words in the shaped grid. Words may be written horizontally, vertically or diagonally and in either a forwards or backwards direction.

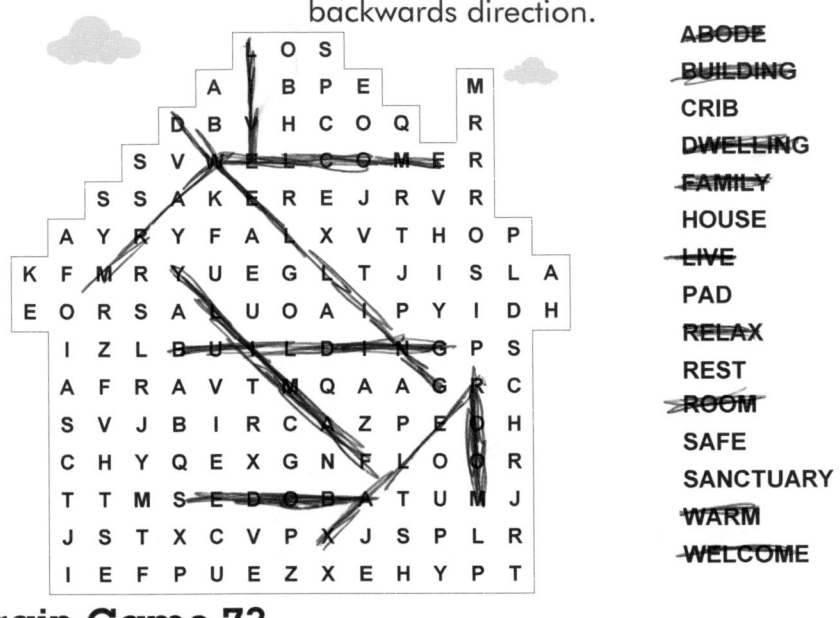

			O	S				
		A	B	P	E		M	
		D	B	H	C	O	Q	R
	S	V	W	E	L	C	O	M E R
	S	S	A	K	E	R	E	J R V R
A	Y	R	Y	F	A	L	X	V T H O P
K F	M	R	Y	U	E	G	L	T J I S L A
E O	R	S	A	U	O	A	I	P Y I D H
	I	Z	L	B	U	I	L	D I N G P S
	A	F	R	A	V	T	M	Q A A G R C
	S	V	J	B	I	R	C	A Z P E D H
	C	H	Y	Q	E	X	G	N F L O R
	T	T	M	S	E	D	O	B A T U M J
	J	S	T	X	C	V	P	X J S P L R
	I	E	F	P	U	E	Z	X E H Y P T

ABODE
BUILDING
CRIB
DWELLING
FAMILY
HOUSE
LIVE
PAD
RELAX
REST
ROOM
SAFE
SANCTUARY
WARM
WELCOME

Brain Game 73

BARK

DOGS

Move from the word at the top of the ladder to the word at the bottom of the ladder by changing one letter on each step of the ladder. Do not rearrange the order of the letters. There may be more than one way of doing this.

Look at the grid below for 15 seconds then cover it up and try to answer the following questions.

1- Name the animals across the top row from left to right.

2- Name the animals across the bottom row from right to left.

3- How many dogs are there in total?

4- Name the animals in the four corners moving left to right, top to bottom.

Cover the grid with a piece of paper. If this isn't possible, maybe a friend can ask you the questions.

Brain Game 75

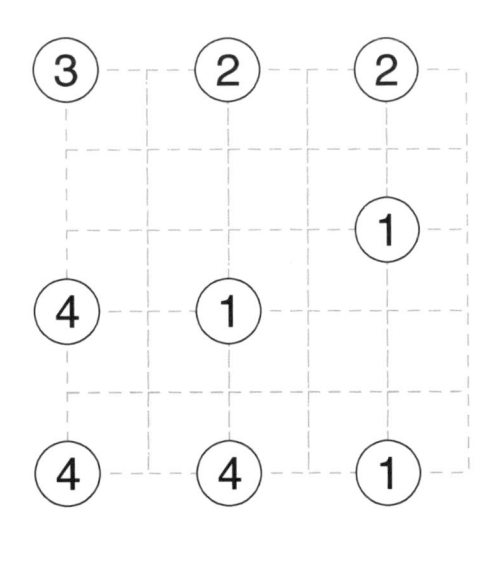

Connect every island (represented by circles) into a single interconnected group. To do this draw bridges between islands. The number in each circle states how many bridges must be connected to that island. Bridges cannot cross each other, can only be drawn horizontally or vertically, and there can be a maximum of two bridges between any pair of islands.

Brain Game 76

Find the words in the shaped grid. Words may be written horizontally, vertically or diagonally and in either a forwards or backwards direction.

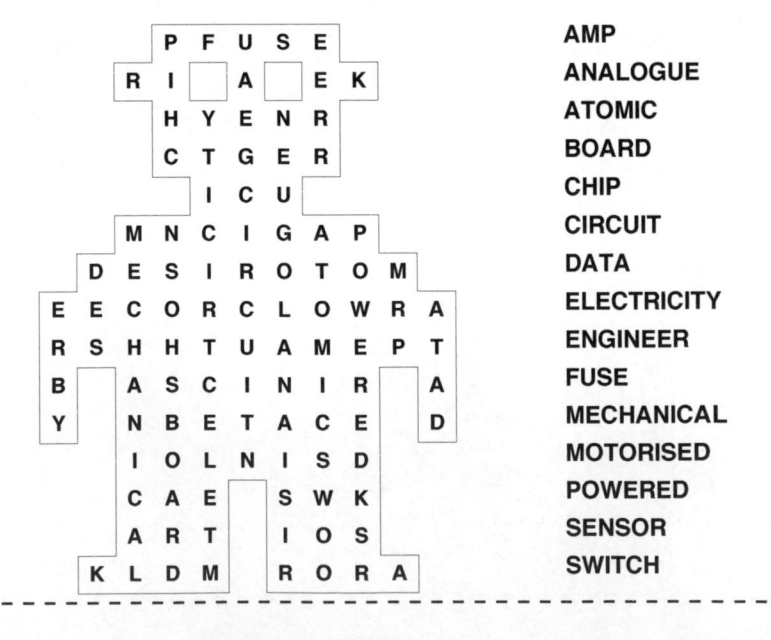

AMP
ANALOGUE
ATOMIC
BOARD
CHIP
CIRCUIT
DATA
ELECTRICITY
ENGINEER
FUSE
MECHANICAL
MOTORISED
POWERED
SENSOR
SWITCH

Brain Game 77

Using the colour key below, fill in the image to create a completed image.

Colour 1: Orange   Colour 2: Black   Colour 3: Red   Colour 4: Green

	4	4																	
	4																		
	4	4										1	1	1	1	1			
		4	4								1	1	1	1	2	1	1	1	
			4							1	1	2	2	1	1	1	1		
		4	4		1	1	1	1	1	1	1	2	2	1	1	1	1		
	4	4		1	1	1	1	1	1	2	1	1	2	2	1	1			
	4	4		1	1	1	1	1	1	2	2	1	1	2	2	1			
	4	4		1	1	1	1	1	1	1	2	2	1	1	2	1		4	
	4	4		1	2	2	1	1	1	1	2	2	1	1	1			4	
	4			1	2	2	2	1	1	1	2	2	1	1			4	4	
		4		1	1	1	2	2	1	1	1	1	1				4	4	
	4	4		1	1	1	1	2	2	1	1	1	1				4	4	
4	4			1	1	2	1	1	1	2	2	1	1				4	4	4
4				1	1	2	2	1	1	1	1	1	4					4	4
4	1	1	1		1	1	1	1	1	1	1	1	4	4			4	4	4
4	1	1	1	1	1	1	1						4	4			4	4	4
4	1	1	1	1	1	1	1						4	4			4	4	
4		1	1	1	1	1	1					4	4	4	4			4	4
4			1	1	1	1	1	1				4	4	4	4			4	4	4

Brain Game 78

Shade in the numbers that are divisible by 4. Once complete, you will reveal a 'timely' image!

89	90	86	26	25	59	11	28	16	56	92	40	68	43	83	87	74	46	77	29
39	19	15	40	92	52	4	84	29	30	34	15	40	88	20	48	56	31	7	94
46	76	32	68	52	36	60	76	34	70	14	26	68	52	32	44	92	60	76	39
60	60	92	4	12	36	60	84	66	33	65	59	24	84	80	72	88	64	20	88
80	24	4	64	56	80	64	56	32	40	56	80	64	68	40	36	76	92	48	72
40	8	60	20	64	16	18	50	31	34	14	45	23	18	72	32	56	16	76	64
78	88	44	48	60	85	25	62	1	18	64	70	15	46	30	64	60	92	8	89
38	45	56	96	10	57	40	73	7	6	11	14	95	12	1	54	76	8	45	42
78	34	23	76	82	95	27	93	55	51	12	31	63	25	9	86	88	27	89	38
83	37	8	80	43	41	3	29	11	26	80	11	35	7	70	71	96	20	11	81
58	21	16	94	66	68	5	28	16	32	92	55	7	3	36	43	30	96	67	58
27	63	84	29	5	67	11	87	26	14	34	10	46	41	6	54	18	24	14	83
86	78	76	40	49	47	22	93	9	37	77	10	83	51	6	49	80	72	77	65
23	82	69	64	57	34	84	61	39	15	5	15	53	24	82	67	96	18	51	17
55	31	46	48	48	29	11	55	53	15	62	11	55	26	69	96	52	58	7	73
13	81	49	9	72	40	10	1	11	38	64	19	85	50	84	16	53	73	89	71
19	63	42	57	39	36	76	58	70	78	13	63	79	20	76	9	43	95	70	82
81	27	95	35	31	63	64	8	8	4	48	84	64	36	55	50	43	47	77	89
7	49	43	94	41	84	3	65	6	21	37	31	57	43	16	79	70	85	82	31
27	1	27	50	44	38	87	55	87	11	93	34	1	89	38	88	35	27	21	78

Connect all dots from number 1 onwards.

Brain Game 80

Fill the grid with the number sequences given in the list. A few have been placed to start you off.

```
      [ ] 6  2 [ ]    [ ]    [ ]
[ ][ ][ ]5 [ ]3 [ ][ ][ ][ ][ ]
      [ ]9  0 [ ]    [ ]    [ ]
[ ][ ][ ]5 [ ]0 [ ]    [ ][ ][ ]
      [ ]7  8 [ ]    [ ]    [ ]
[ ][ ][ ]1 [ ]8 [ ]   [ ][ ][ ][ ]
      [ ]   1  [ ]3         [ ]
[ ][ ][ ][ ]  [ ] 2 [ ][ ][ ][ ]
      [ ]  [ ]  [ ]1   [ ]
[ ][ ][ ]   [ ][ ]7 [ ][ ][ ][ ]
      [ ]  [ ]  [ ]6   [ ]
6 3 1 2 7 0 2 9 8 2 3 4 5
      [ ]  [ ]  [ ]5   [ ]  [ ]
```

4 numbers	**6 numbers**	**8 numbers**
2241	121724	14771821
6982	497645	53781790
7261	551122	79696935
9621	~~659571~~	81158013

5 numbers	**7 numbers**	**13 numbers**
16953	1231307	4275935779236
51208	~~2300881~~	~~6312702982345~~
65574	~~3217695~~	
87535	3741887	

Brain Game 81

Complete exercises a-c in order to work out how much change you have left.

a) Add up the total amount of money available to spend.
b) Calculate the total of the shopping.
c) Work out the change left over once any valid offers have been applied.

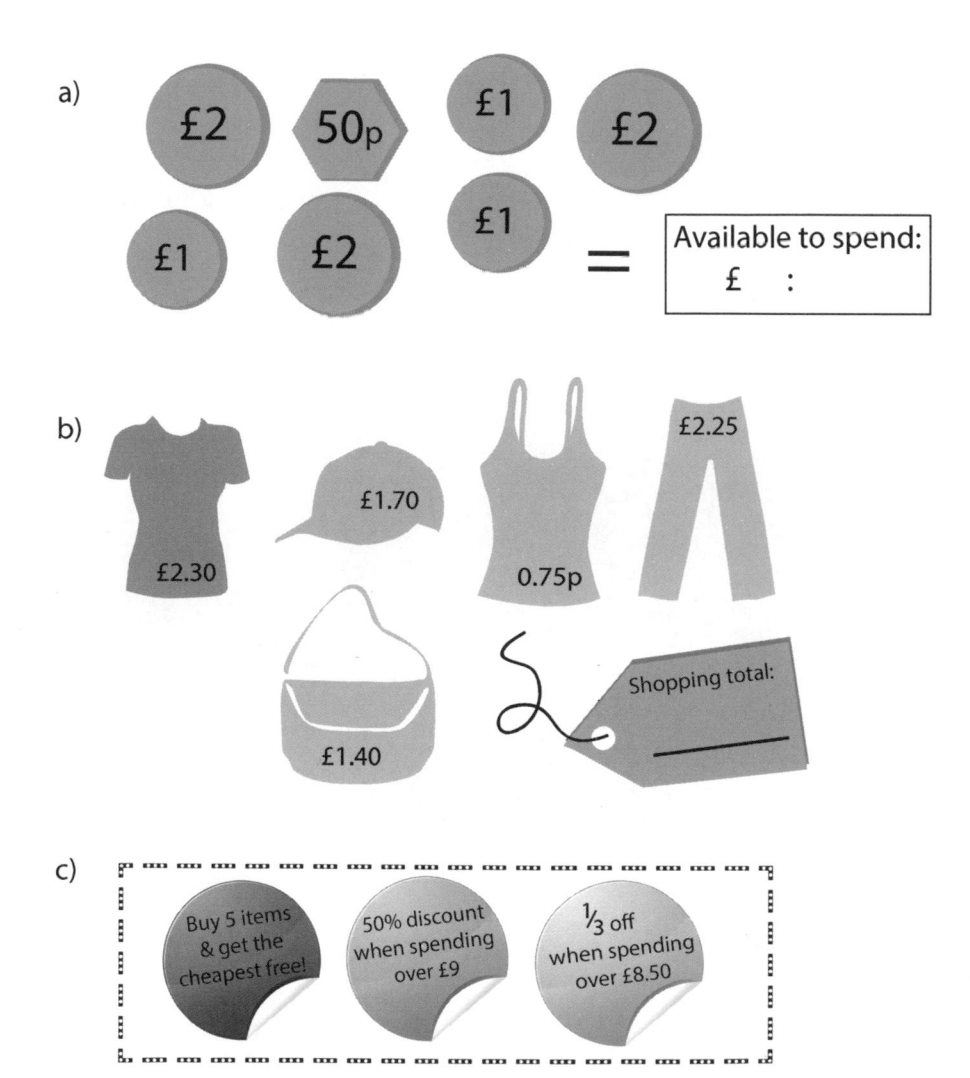

a)

£2 50p £1 £2

£1 £2 £1

= Available to spend:
£   :

b)

£2.30 £1.70 £2.25

0.75p

£1.40

Shopping total:
_____

c)

Buy 5 items & get the cheapest free!

50% discount when spending over £9

⅓ off when spending over £8.50

= Change left over
£   :

Brain Game 82

21			**24**
			23
25	**31**		**20**
		29	

Complete the magic square so that the total of the numbers in each row, column and the two diagonals is **94**.

Each number from **16-31** appears once in the grid.

Brain Game 83

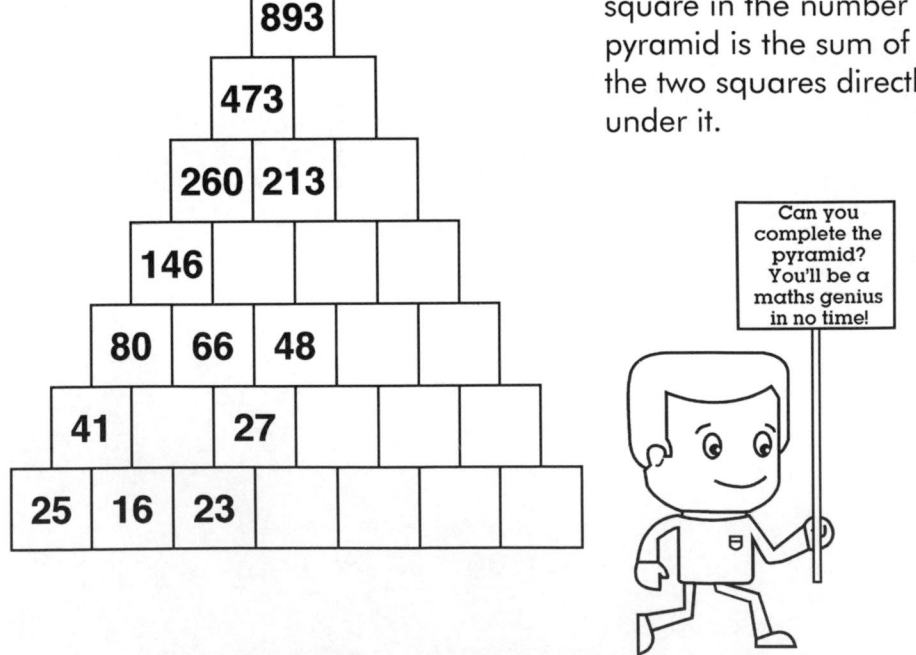

The value of each square in the number pyramid is the sum of the two squares directly under it.

Can you complete the pyramid? You'll be a maths genius in no time!

Brain Game 84

Each number represents a different letter of the alphabet. In this puzzle, the 11 represents a V for example. Complete the grid by working out what the other numbers represent.

3		6		19				7		21		19
21	16	2	6	20	1		21	4	20	3	4	20
16		5		6		10		9		20		6
20	21	22	6	10	10	21		9	21	24	2	9
16		21		23		9		26		10		19
6	24	25	19		24	2	25	1	12			
5		5		2		24		16		1		8
		15	4	24	20	1		18	5	20	14
19		19		13		24		6		1		21
20	21	3	6	13		11	24	19	24	22	26	1
6		6		26		1		14		16		11
20	24	10	23	1	20		22	1	17	21	16	1
1		1		19				19		8		16

A B C D E F G H I J K L M N O P Q R S T U V W X Y Z

1	2	3	4	5	6	7	8	9	10	11	12	13
	N									V	X	

14	15	16	17	18	19	20	21	22	23	24	25	26
	Q		F	M			O					L

Brain Game 85

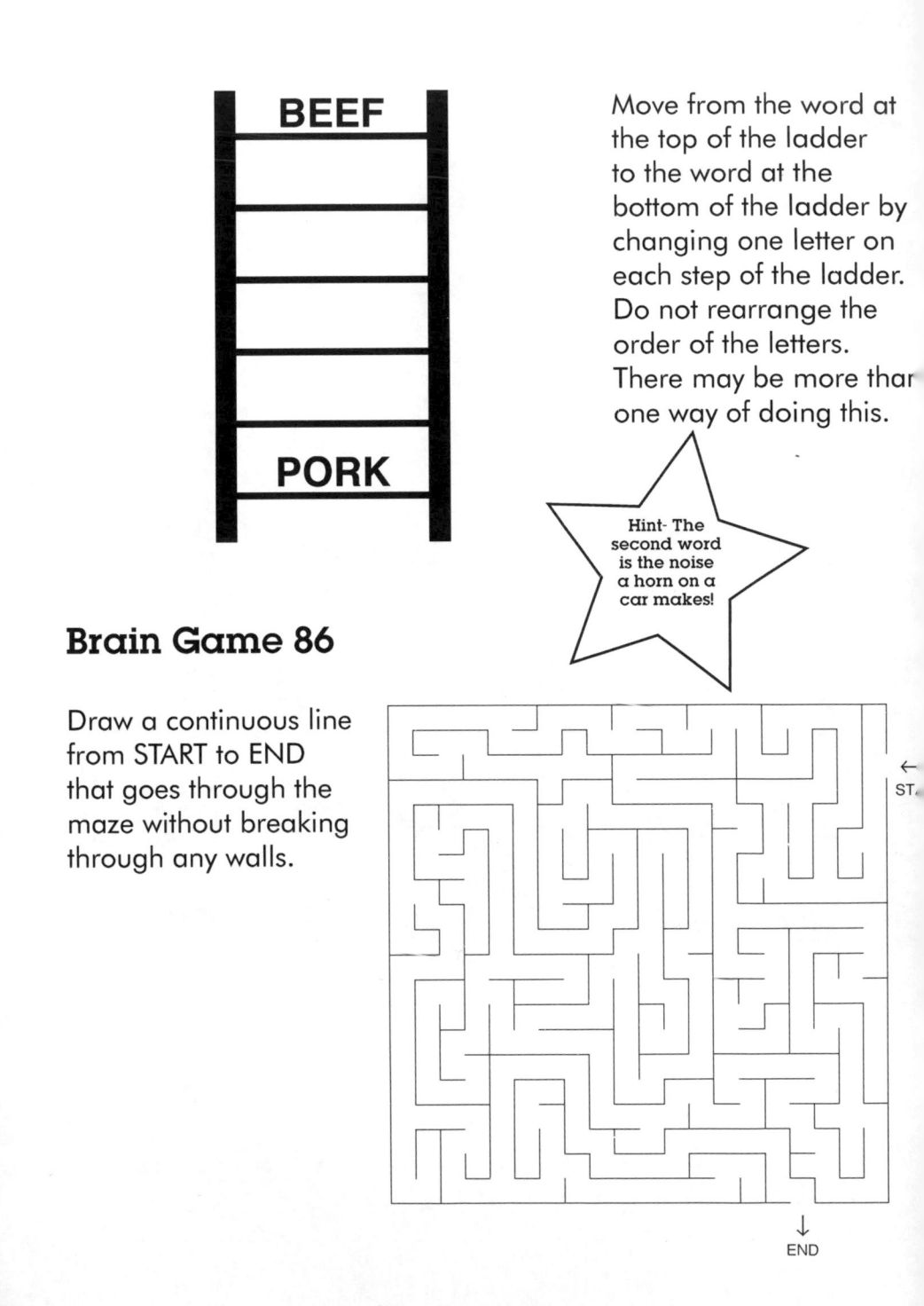

BEEF

PORK

Move from the word at the top of the ladder to the word at the bottom of the ladder by changing one letter on each step of the ladder. Do not rearrange the order of the letters. There may be more than one way of doing this.

Hint- The second word is the noise a horn on a car makes!

Brain Game 86

Draw a continuous line from START to END that goes through the maze without breaking through any walls.

← ST.

↓
END

Brain Game 87

Using the colour key below, fill in the image to create a completed image.

Colour 1: Red   Colour 2: Green   Colour 3: Light brown   Colour 4: Black

2	2	2	2	2	2	2	2	2	2	2	2	2							
2	2	2	2	2	2	2	2	1	2	2	2	2	2						
2	2	1	2	2	2	2	2	2	2	2	2	2	2	2					
2	2	2	2	2	2	1	2	2	2	2	2	1	2	2					
2	2	2	2	2	2	2	2	2	2	2	2	2	2	2					
2	2	2	2	2	2	2	2	2	1	2	2	2	2	2					
2	2	2	2	1	2	2	2	2	2	2	2	2	2						
2	1	2	2	2	2	2	2	2	2	2	2	3							
2	2	2	2	2	2	2	1	2	2	2		3							
2	2	2	2	2	2	2	2	2	2			3							
2	2	2	3									3							
3	3	3	3									3							
3	3	3	3								4	4	4						
3	3	3								4	4		4	4	4				
3	3	3								4	4		4	4					
3	3	3								4	4		4	4					
3	3	3								4	4		4	4	4				
3	3	3									4		4	4					
3	3	3	3	2	2	2	2	2	2	2	2	2	2	2	2	2	2	2	2
3	3	3	3	3	3	2	2	2	2	2	2	2	2	2	2	2	2	2	2

Brain Game 88

			19
15	17		
	16	11	
	7		14

Complete the magic square so that the total of the numbers in each row, column and the two diagonals is 50.

Each number from 5-20 appears once in the grid.

Brain Game 89

		3			2
		2	6	3	
		6		4	
	4		2		
	3	4	5		
5			3		

Place each number from 1-6 exactly once in each of the 6 horizontal rows and the 6 vertical columns. In addition each 2x3 bold-lined region of cells must contain the numbers from 1-6 exactly once.

Moving from one letter to another, can you find a path that visits every square and spells each of the words listed under the puzzle? Start on the shaded square.

S	T	M	A	R	K	C	O	N	E
Y	E	P	Y	S	E	T	L	O	L
R	P	U	A	E	T	S	N	O	C
E	P	D	R	U	R	C	H	C	O
N	E	I	R	N	O	T	T	U	A
I	C	U	A	P	A	H	H	O	R
F	R	B	S	S	I	S	A	E	H
G	I	E	U	F	M	L	D	D	A
N	E	I	E	L	S	I	N	E	N
I	F	T	E	E	W	S	R	E	C

Briefing, Coauthor, Colonel, Construes, Cuirass, Dancer, Finery, Fuels, Headline, Mishap, Notch, Steppe, Sweetie, Upmarket, Yard

Brain Game 91

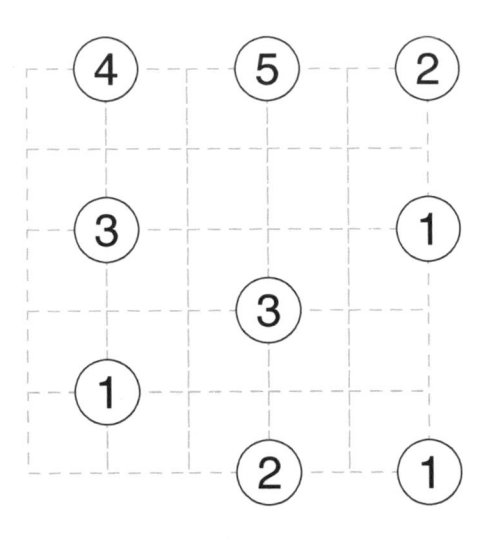

Connect every island (represented by circles) into a single interconnected group. To do this draw bridges between islands. The number in each circle states how many bridges must be connected to that island. Bridges cannot cross each other, can only be drawn horizontally or vertically, and there can be a maximum of two bridges between any pair of islands.

Brain Game 92

	-		x	5	-25
+	■	÷	■	+	
	+		-		8
-	■	+	■	+	
	x		÷	2	28
3		10		11	

Enter the numbers from 1 - 9 once each into the puzzle grid, so as to complete the maths sums that read across and down the puzzle grid. Perform sums from left to right and top to bottom.

Connect all dots from number 1 onwards.

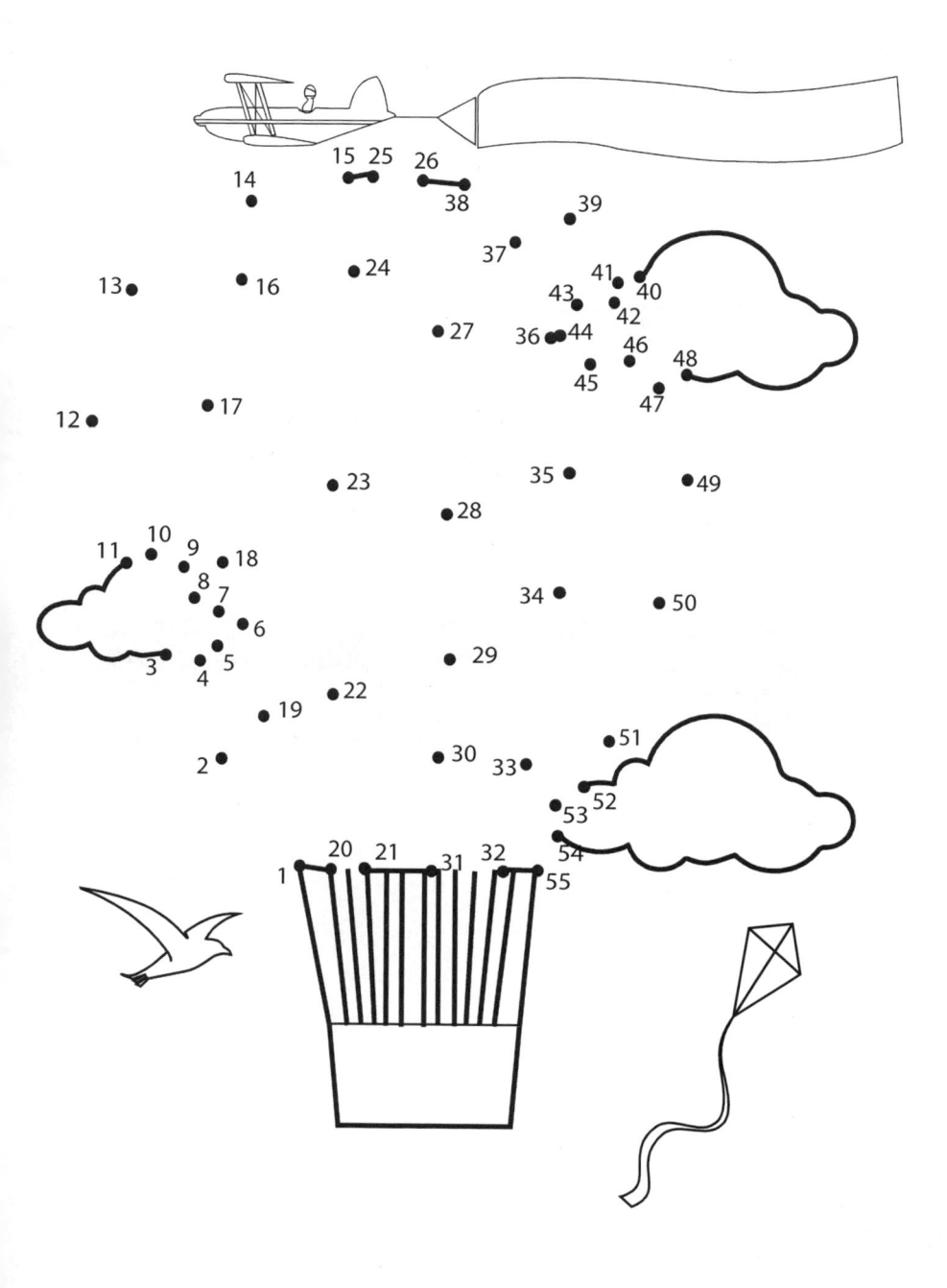

Brain Game 94

Complete the crossword clues to fill the grid.

Across

1 - Time when you are young (9)

6 - Love dearly (5)

7 - Regulations (5)

9 - Error (7)

12 - Primates (7)

16 - Eg oaks and beeches (5)

17 - Prepared for (5)

18 - Cuddly toy (5,4)

Down

2 - Metal (4)

3 - What one often does when asleep (5)

4 - Mythical giants (5)

5 - American currency (6)

6 - Try to do something (7)

8 - Background on a theatre stage (7)

10 - Very cold (3)

11 - Put inside (6)

13 - Became less intense or less difficult (5)

14 - Feeling regret (5)

15 - Stare (4)

Place the numbers 1-6 exactly once per row, column and 2x3 bold-lined box. In addition the numbers 1-6 must appear exactly once in the two main diagonals, marked in grey.

		6	4		
1					5
6					4
2					3
3					2
		2	3		

Answer the clues to the right of each row. The answers will read the same horizontally and vertically.

Jack and ____ : nursery rhyme

Thought or suggestion

Opposite of more

Ultimate

Brain Game 97

Each number represents a different letter of the alphabet. In this puzzle, the 3 represents a B for example. Complete the grid by working out what the other numbers represent.

	6		5		11		14		22		12	
22	19	15	4	21	19		26	11	19	1	23	20
	23		12		15		19		2		18	
25	1	1	22		17	19	12	16	19	9	4	15
			23		9		7		15		13	
1	3	2	8	1	4	14		24	1	7	19	22
	4		15		15		15		17		10	
19	14	14	12	20		26	19	23	13	8	26	19
	8		26		24		26		19			
8	10	26	19	23	19	14	26		10	1	23	13
	19		23		25		4		26		12	
19	14	16	12	17	19		16	11	12	10	16	19
	14		15		15		19		15		19	

A B C D E F G H I J K L M N O P Q R S T U V W X Y Z

1	2	3	4	5	6	7	8	9	10	11	12	13
	V	B						F				

14	15	16	17	18	19	20	21	22	23	24	25	26
	L	C		G						J	W	

Connect every island (represented by circles) into a single interconnected group. To do this draw bridges between islands. The number in each circle states how many bridges must be connected to that island. Bridges cannot cross each other, can only be drawn horizontally or vertically, and there can be a maximum of two bridges between any pair of islands.

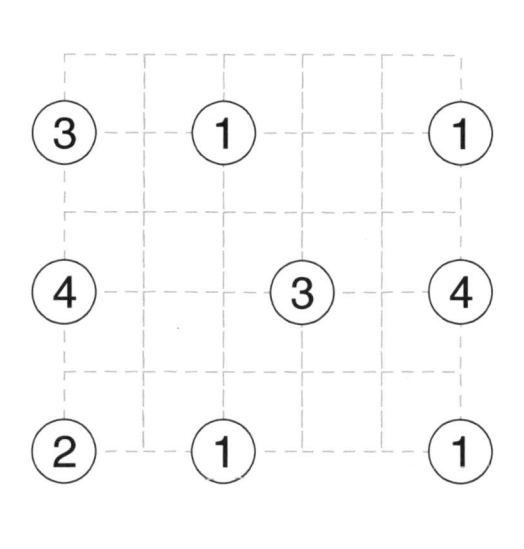

The value of each square in the number pyramid is the sum of the two squares directly under it.

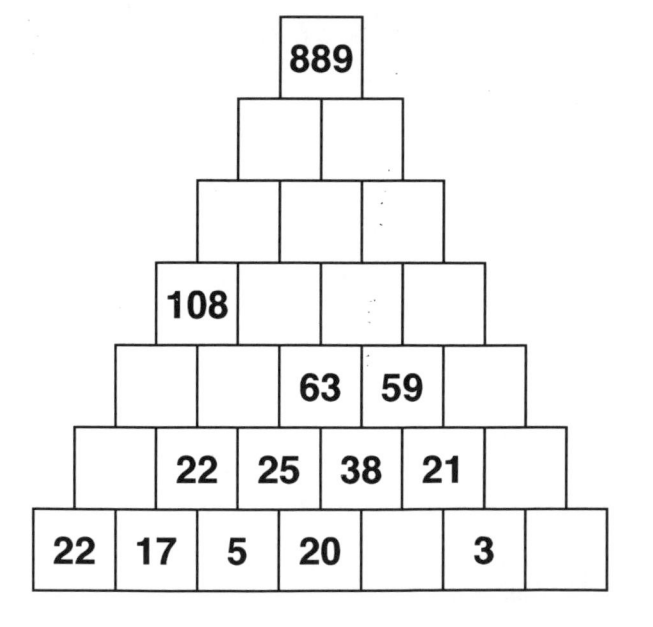

Brain Game 100

Moving from one letter to another, can you find a path that visits every square and spells each of the words listed under the puzzle? Start on the shaded square.

A	N	S	R	T	O	S	H	P	A
B	D	S	E	H	M	S	B	I	R
L	R	T	A	N	D	D	E	L	G
E	A	H	E	S	D	O	W	I	O
P	Y	C	T	S	B	N	N	T	T
O	R	N	E	I	O	U	Y	Y	O
T	C	A	D	S	U	N	P	P	H
F	A	R	B	E	R	D	E	R	T
S	A	S	E	N	I	R	H	S	A
I	T	N	U	A	C	R	U	N	I

Bandstand, Branches, Debility, Downy, Hurricane, Pearl, Pertains, Photographs, Resisted, Smothers, Unbound, Unsatisfactory

Solutions

No. 1

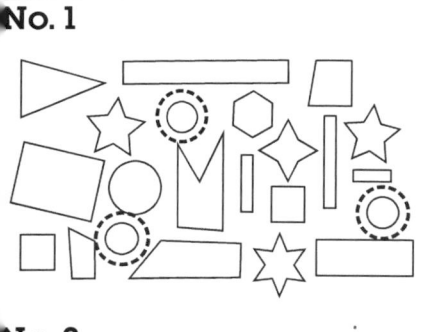

No. 2

Matching key - 5

No. 3

No. 4

Kite maze - C

No. 5

No. 6

Reflection - A

No. 7

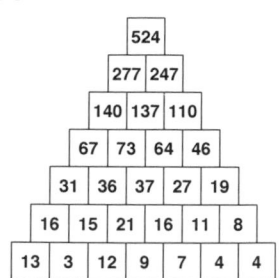

No. 8

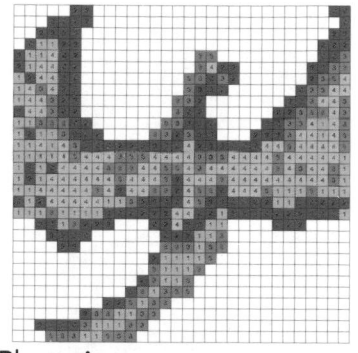

Phoenix

No. 9

The nine letter word is:
Automated

No. 10

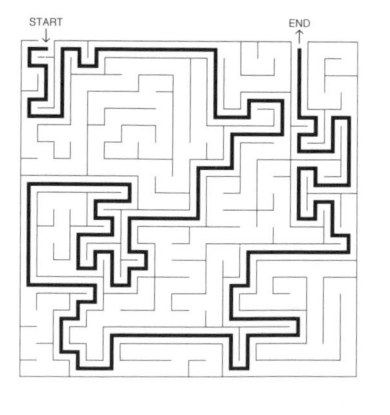

Solutions

No. 11

3	2	6	4	1	5
1	4	5	2	3	6
6	1	2	5	4	3
5	3	4	6	2	1
4	5	1	3	6	2
2	6	3	1	5	4

No. 12
Animal maths - 170

No. 13
Time exericse - B5, C1, D2, E4

No. 14

No. 15
Guess the phrase -
A round of applause

No. 16

No. 17

No. 18
Money left - £1.55

No. 19

12	9	22	15
16	21	10	11
17	20	7	14
13	8	19	18

No. 20
The nine letter word is:
Collected

No. 21
Anagram connect - Phased

No. 22
Silhouette puzzle - B

No. 23

3	1	5	2	4	6
2	6	4	1	3	5
1	4	6	3	5	2
5	3	2	6	1	4
6	5	3	4	2	1
4	2	1	5	6	3

No. 24

```
              904
          498   406
       273   225   181
    146   127   98   83
   77  69  58  40  43
  43  34  35  23  17  26
22  21  13  22  1  16  10
```

No. 25

No. 26
Rotation - D

No. 27

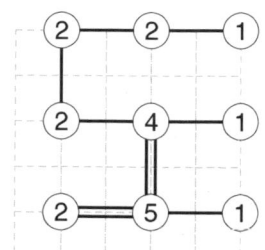

No. 28

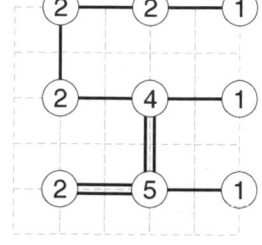

No. 29
Matching key - 6

No. 30

2	x	3	÷	6	1
-		+		-	
8	-	4	x	9	36
-		÷		-	
1	x	7	x	5	35
-7		1		-8	

Solutions

No. 31

2	9	8	4	3	5	3	2	1	7	8	9
6		7		9			6				1
0		1	7	3	1	2	8	6		9	0
3		6		5		4		9		4	6
5	5	8	5		8	2	1	5	4	1	4
3		5		9		4		0		2	1
5	6	6	8	9			6	0	5	0	0
3		0		7	8	8		6	8		5
4		5	0	5	9	6	6		8	8	5
9		7		6		5		1		3	9
7		4		2	9	7	5	3	6	6		2
2				2				6		7	6
	8	9	0	2	1	4	1	4	3	0	1	0

No. 32

4	2	1	6	3	5
5	3	6	4	2	1
2	1	5	3	6	4
3	6	4	1	5	2
1	5	3	2	4	6
6	4	2	5	1	3

No. 33

No. 34
Folded paper -
CELEBRATION
HOLIDAYS

No. 35

0	0	1	1	0	1
1	0	1	1	0	0
0	1	0	0	1	1
1	1	0	1	0	0
0	0	1	0	1	1
1	1	0	0	1	0

No. 36
Matching pairs - AC, DF, BE

No. 37
Animal maths - 30

No. 38

S	I	N	K
I	R	O	N
N	O	S	E
K	N	E	E

No. 39

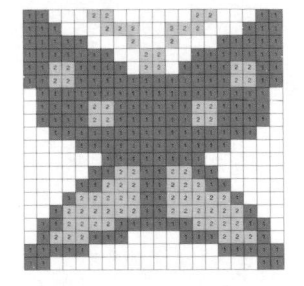

No. 40
Object split - '4'

Solutions

No. 41
The next letter in the sequence
is: B
'Can You Work Out The Next
Letter In The Sequence BELOW'

No. 42

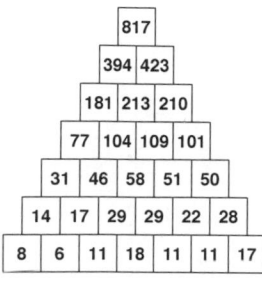

			817			
		394	423			
	181	213	210			
77	104	109	101			
31	46	58	51	50		
14	17	29	29	22	28	
8	6	11	18	11	11	17

No. 43

Panda

No. 44

14	18	13	17
9	21	10	22
16	12	19	15
23	11	20	8

No. 45
Word finder - Spring

No. 46
The nine letter word is:
Condition

No. 47
Guess the phrase -
Black hole

No. 48

	3		5		2		5		5		9	
7	3	5	9	1	5	6	5	6	9	5	4	5
	3		0		4		8		6		6	
9	4	4	7	5	7	1	5		2	9	3	3
			0		8		9		7		4	
1	3	4	2	1	9	0		4	4	7	7	5
	1				2		7				1	
4	3	8	8	0		1	0	0	2	1	8	4
	0		1		1		4		3			
2	2	0	6		3	2	3	2	9	2	8	0
	1		0		9		7		2		4	
4	9	4	8	9	5	5	5	8	9	0	2	6	4
	4		7		5		8		2		0	

No. 49

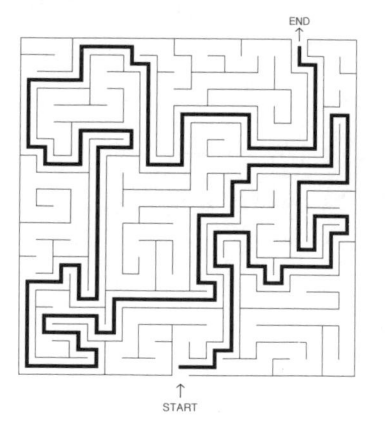

END ↑

↑
START

No. 50
Object split - 'R'

Solutions

No. 51
Folded paper -
UNICORN
JEWELLERY
ORCHESTRA

No. 52
Riddle- I am a 'SMILE'

No. 53

4	6	2	1	3	5
3	5	1	2	4	6
2	4	3	6	5	1
6	1	5	4	2	3
1	3	4	5	6	2
5	2	6	3	1	4

No. 54

19	8	11	30	17	2
10	31	18	1	12	29
7	20	9	34	3	16
32	35	24	15	28	13
21	6	33	26	23	4
36	25	22	5	14	27

No. 55
Money left - £1.97

No. 56

No. 57

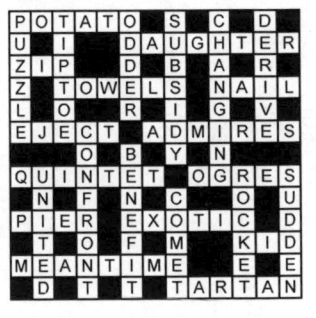

FEEL
PEEL
PEEK
PECK
PICK
SICK

No. 58

P	O	T	A	T	O		S		C		D	
U		I		D	A	U	G	H	T	E	R	
Z	I	P		D		B		A		R		
Z		T	O	W	E	L	S		N	A	I	L
L		O		R		I		G		V		
E	J	E	C	T		A	D	M	I	R	E	S
		O		B		Y		N				
Q	U	I	N	T	E	T		O	G	R	E	S
	N		F		N		C		O		U	
P	I	E	R		E	X	O	T	I	C		D
	T		O		F		M		K	I	D	
M	E	A	N	T	I	M	E			E		E
	D		T		T		T	A	R	T	A	N

No. 59

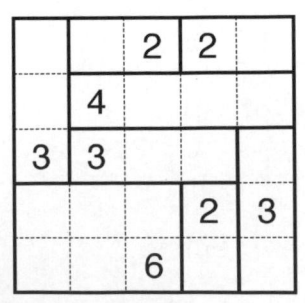

Solutions

No. 60
Animal maths - 47

No. 61

	1		4		7		7		2		1	
6	0	9	6	1	6	0	7	4	9	3	6	6
	3		7		4		5		0		2	
3	4	0	7	5	3	9	2		7	9	5	5
			9		4		0		7		2	
4	3	2	4	9	6	7		6	3	8	0	4
	6				6		6				2	
1	0	0	7	3		3	8	6	6	9	3	8
	6		4		5		7		8			
7	5	8	2		7	2	5	5	9	6	8	5
	5		7		3		6		9		7	
6	4	4	8	5	8	0	9	8	8	9	3	7
	4		9		8		4		2		2	

No. 62

No. 63
The nine letter word is:
Marmalade

No. 64

No. 65
Scales - 12 squares

No. 66

17	16	12	5
6	11	15	18
7	10	14	19
20	13	9	8

No. 67
Anagram connect - Roasts

No. 68

C	H	E	F
H	I	L	L
E	L	S	E
F	L	E	E

No. 69

Solutions

No. 70

2	+	3	÷	5	1
x		+		x	
4	x	9	-	6	30
÷		x		+	
8	-	1	-	7	0
1		12		37	

No. 71

```
H O O P L A   S   P   A
E   U   N E C K L A C E
A R T   G   O   A   I
V   F I A S C O   T I D Y
E   I   T   T   F   I
N O T E S   R E J O I C E
    N   B   R   R
M E N T I O N   A M A Z E
  D   R   U   R   B   X
D I V A   Q U A V E R   I
  T   N   U   V   O W L
C O N C R E T E   A   E
  R   E   T   N E E D E D
```

No. 72

```
      L O S
    A I B P E       M
  D B V H C O Q     R
 S V W E L C O M E R R
 S S A K E R E J R V R
A Y R Y F A L X V T H O P
K F M R Y U E G L T J I S L A
E O R S A L U O A I P Y I D H
 I Z L B U I L D I N G P S
 A F R A V T M Q A A G R C
 S V J B I R C A Z P E O H
 C H Y Q E X G N F L O O R
 T T M S E D O B A T U M J
 J S T X C V P X J S P L R
 I E F P U E Z X E H Y P T
```

No. 73

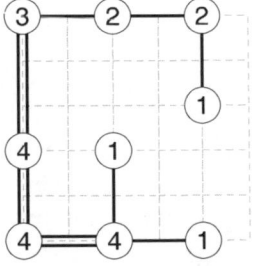

BARK
BARS
BAGS
HAGS
HOGS
DOGS

No. 74
Memory test:
1- dog, goat, penguin
2 - rabbit, dog, penguin
3 - 3 dogs
4 - dog, penguin, penguin, rabbit

No. 75

No. 76

```
      P F U S E
  R   I   A   E K
  H   Y E N   R
  C   T G E   R
      I C U
  M N C I G A P
 D E S I R O T O M
E E C O R C L O W R A
R S H A R T U A M E P T A
B   N S C I N A C   E   A
Y   B E T A   M I   R   D
    O L N I S D
    I C A T   S W K
    C A R T   I O S
  K L D M   R O R A
```

Solutions

No. 77

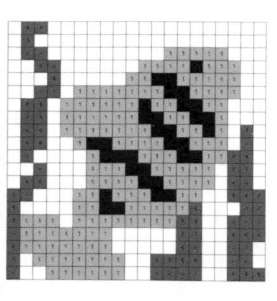

No. 78

No. 79

No. 80

7		6		2		8		4		5
4	2	7	5	9	3	5	7	7	9	2	3	6
6		9		0		5		7		7
8	1	1	5	8	0	1	3		6	9	8	2
		7		8		5		4		1
3	7	4	1	8	8	7		6	5	5	7	4
9				1		3				9
1	6	9	5	3		1	2	3	1	3	0	7
9		5		5		1		2
9	6	2	1		1	4	7	7	1	8	2	1
9		1		2		6		7		2
6	3	1	2	7	0	2	9	8	2	3	4	5
5		2		8		5		4		1

No. 81
Money exercise:
1a - £9.50
b - £8.40
c - £1.85

No. 82

21	19	30	24
26	28	17	23
25	31	18	20
22	16	29	27

No. 83

					893					
				473		420				
			260		213		207			
		146		114		99		108		
	80		66		48		51		57	
41		39		27		21		30		27
25	16	23	4	17	13	14

No. 84

Solutions

No. 85

| BEEF |
| BEEP |
| PEEP |
| PEEK |
| PERK |
| PORK |

No. 86

No. 87

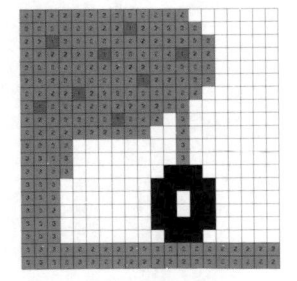

No. 88

8	10	13	19
15	17	6	12
18	16	11	5
9	7	20	14

No. 89

6	1	3	4	5	2
4	5	2	6	3	1
3	2	6	1	4	5
1	4	5	2	6	3
2	3	4	5	1	6
5	6	1	3	2	4

No. 90

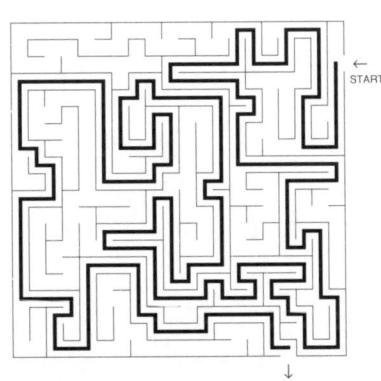

No. 91

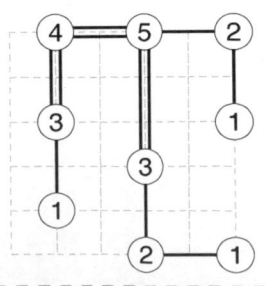

No. 92

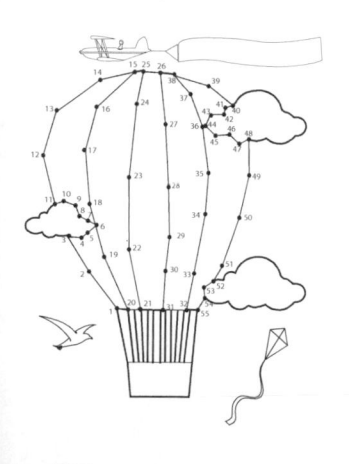

1	-	6	x	5	-25
+		÷		+	
9	+	3	-	4	8
-		+		+	
7	x	8	÷	2	28
3		10		11	

No. 93

No. 94

No. 95

5	3	6	4	2	1
1	2	4	6	3	5
6	1	3	2	5	4
2	4	5	1	6	3
3	6	1	5	4	2
4	5	2	3	1	6

No. 96

J	I	L	L
I	D	E	A
L	E	S	S
L	A	S	T

No. 97

```
  Z Q H   S D   A
D E L U X E   T H E O R Y
  R   A   L   E V   G
W O O D   P E A C E F U L
      R   F   K   L   M
O B V I O U S   J O K E D
  U   L   L   P   N
E S S A Y   T E R M I T E
  I   T   J   T   E
I N T E R E S T   N O R M
  E   R   W   U   T A
E S C A P E   C H A N C E
  S   L   L   E   L   E
```

No. 98

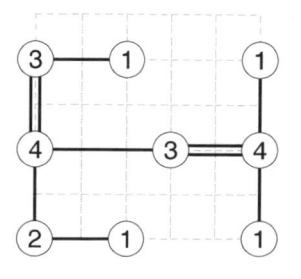

Solutions

No. 99

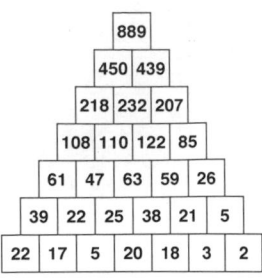

```
                    889
                 450   439
              218   232   207
           108   110   122   85
         61   47   63   59   26
      39   22   25   38   21   5
   22   17   5   20   18   3   2
```

No. 100

```
A N S R T O S H P A
B D S E H M S B I R
L R T A N D D E L G
E A H E S D O W I O
P Y C T S B N N T T
O R N E I O U Y Y O
T C A D S U N P P H
F A R B E R D E R T
S A S E N I R H S A
I T N U A C R U N I
```